Contents

Teacher's Notes

Some 14 million people are refugees in today's world and another 25 million people are internally displaced within their own country. The migration of refugees is a growing challenge to governments, NGOs and international agencies - the numbers of refugees has doubled in a decade. Even in the UK the numbers of refugees has increased substantially since the mid 1980s. Almost every London school now has refugee students, something that could not have been predicted ten years ago.

The word refugee is now part of everyday vocabulary. But it does have a precise legal meaning. A person with refugee status is defined someone who has fled from his or her home country or is unable to return to it *'owing to a well founded fear of being persecuted for reasons of race, religion, nationality, membership of a particular social group or political opinion.'* (From the 1951 UN Convention and 1967 Protocol Relating to the Status of refugees). An asylum-seeker is a person who has crossed an international border in search of safety, and refugee status, in another country.

Television and newspapers have brought the experiences of refugees into everybody's sitting rooms. Sadly, the media portrayal of refugees, particularly in the British tabloid and local press, often increases popular misconceptions and prejudices. Even young children may pick up on these popular misconceptions, and the racist bullying of refugee children is an all too common occurrence in European schools. One of the aims in writing this book was to challenge children's misconceptions and prejudices about refugees, and thus make refugee children feel more welcome in their new homes.

Aims of the book

❥ to explore themes such as human rights, justice, identity and how we treat newcomers;
❥ to help children to gain a greater understanding of the flight of refugees and their needs in a new society;
❥ to help children see that they are linked to other nations through migration;
❥ to develop greater empathy to refugees, locally, nationally and internationally;
❥ to help children see that refugees are ordinary people like themselves, but with extraordinary recent experiences;
❥ to encourage positive attitudes towards cultural diversity and to help children challenge prejudice and racist behaviour in their own environments;
❥ to help children act to support refugees, locally, nationally and internationally.

Methodology

The information, testimonies and activities are aimed at primary school children, but not all the written information is suitable for reading by younger children. Instead it may be read to children.

The written information and testimonies are all written for children themselves to read. All the activities have teacher/group leader instructions.

The Picture Set

A set of photographs and drawings accompany the book. The two children's drawings are to be used as stimulus for the activity on page 42 in Chapter Three. The photographs can also be used to stimulate discussion.

One activity that can be used with the picture set is to get children to write captions for the photographs to illustrate what they think is shown in each photograph. This can then be compared with the real photographic caption, shown below.

1. A Turkish Kurdish child's drawings of police breaking up a demonstration.
2. A Sri Lankan Tamil child's drawing of bombing of her home village by the Sri Lankan air force.
3. A Tutsi boy from Rwanda who became separated from his parents while they were fleeing Rwanda. He was then attacked. Now he lives in a children's home in Congo for unaccompanied and orphaned refugee children. The children's home is run by UNICEF which is also trying to trace this boy's parents. Photograph by Howard Davies.
4. A well at a Sierra Leonean refugee camp in Liberia. Clean water is an immediate necessity for refugees. UNHCR.
5. Afghan refugee girls in a school in a refugee camp in Pakistan. UNHCR.
6. Somali refugees tend trees in a nursery near a refugee camp in Ethiopia. The trees will be planted around the camp to provide firewood and prevent soil erosion. The tree nursery also provides work for newly returned Ethiopians who were refugees in other countries. UNHCR.
7. Vietnamese refugees arriving in the UK. Before coming to the UK these refugees had lived in camps in Hong Kong. Howard Davies.
8. An exercise class for older Polish refugees at a sheltered housing project for elderly refugees in London. Maggie Lambert.
9. A dance class run by a Tamil refugee self-help group in the UK. Howard Davies.
10. A Somali class for children run by a refugee self-help group. Karen Robinson.
11. An Iraqi Kurdish girl living in London shows a picture of her father. She has become separated from him. Tim Fox.
12. Mozambican refugees in Malawi collect parcels of food, tools and plastic sheeting, prior to their return to Mozambique. UNHCR.
13. A peace education class in Burundi where Hutu and Tutsi children meet, talk and try and work together to make peace. Howard Davies.
14. Refugee children and their friends in a south London school. The children worked together to collect and write stories. The stories, from all over the world, were collected and published in a book. The book was launched and the local newspaper invited. South London Press.

A game board also accompanies this book. This is for use in Chapter Four.

The Curriculum

The information, testimonies and activities can be used in different parts of the school curriculum in England and Wales, Scotland and Northern Ireland. The areas where the material might be used include

English

Literacy hour work
Writing stories and accounts
Interviewing people
Making presentations

History

The growth of multi-ethnic UK
The Second World War
Local history projects
Oral history

Geography
Finding out about other places
Migration and journeys
Links with other countries in an interdependent world

Religious education
Religious festivals
Persecution because of religious beliefs

Art
Looking at art forms from other countries
Using art to represent feelings

Cross curricular themes
Danger and being scared
Loss
Children's rights
Safety
How we treat others
Justice
Identity

Schools With Refugee Students

More and more British schools have refugee students, particularly those in Greater London. Teachers will obviously have to be sensitive to the needs of refugee children, particularly when initiating class projects on refugees.

Refugee children may have experienced traumatic events in their home countries or during their escape. They may have seen members of their family injured, killed or arrested. Such horrific events cannot easily be discussed in classrooms.

Refugee children may also not want to talk about their home country or family circumstances because they are worried about family left at home, or because they feel that it might jeopardise their chances of staying in Britain, or eventually returning home. Refugee children may not want to discuss their circumstances because they do not want to feel different from other children. And they may feel embarrassed about the popular images of their home country. For example, some Somali children in British schools have felt unable to admit they were from Somalia because the only image their teachers and fellow pupils has of Somalia was that of famine and war.

But there are many ways of making refugee students feel secure, while at the same time increasing knowledge about their home countries. Displays about life in students' countries of origin are one way. Schools can also invite parents and members of refugee communities to talk to students. All school work on refugees must seek to humanise those who flee, and to enable non-refugee students to feel empathy towards refugee students.

Teaching about controversial issues

Sometimes teachers are afraid to tackle issues like the movement and reception of refugees because they are controversial and may require a lot of knowledge to understand them. Teachers may assume that they must solve or at least confront the problems in advance of presenting them to children. This is not easy when issues are contestable and when different opinions can be put forward by different sides. Because of these difficulties, some teachers may ignore controversial issues completely.

This book has been written from the perspective that children should be helped to understand how different opinions are formed. Many of the activities give children the opportunity to explore different opinions, and to explore the complex feelings generated by examining how we receive newcomers in our society.

Chapter One

Introduction

Refugees are people who have fled from their homes in fear. This chapter looks at why people leave their homes and who are today's refugees.

Palestinian refugee children at school in Lebanon. The Palestinians are one of the largest refugee groups. After 50 years there is still no solution that will enable many refugees to rebuild their lives   UNRWA

Refugees are one group of people who have to move home. The first three activities look at the movement or migration of people.

Activity

Moving

Time needed: one hour.
You will need to collect local, national and world maps, drawing pins and small pieces of card. Using the maps, pin the name of each child in the class on the places where they have lived. The activity can be used to prompt discussion on who has moved the furthest or stayed in the same place the longest.

Activity

Family trees

Time needed: two lessons with homework time for research.
You will need to prepare your own family tree on the board or a large piece of paper. Show the class how to construct a family tree, recording names, births, marriages and deaths. For homework, children should research where their family were born and to where they moved during their lives.

The family trees can be used to prompt class discussion on migration and why people might move.

Activity

Why do people move?

Time needed: one hour. You will need some small pieces of paper or 'post-its' and pens.

The class should be divided up into pairs. Each pair should write on a piece of paper or 'post-it' the reasons that people move their homes. Children should include ideas from their own life and abroad.

The class should then come together to make a single list of why people might move home. Then using the list, the class should help sort out the reasons into two column

reasons that people move because they want to	reasons that people move because they are forced to do so

This sorting exercise can be used to introduce the idea that refugees are one group of people who move against their will. Children can then read stories about refugees or view videos such as 'Refugee Children' (*see Further Resources*).

Information

Who are refugees?

Polish refugee children arriving in the UK, 1946

In today's world there are nearly 14 million refugees. They are ordinary people who have fled from their own countries because of war, or because their religion, political beliefs, their ethnic group or way of life puts them in danger of arrest, torture or death.

Another 25 million people have fled from their homes because their lives are in danger, but have gone into hiding in their home country. This group of people are called displaced people. The have fled from their homes for the same reasons as refugees. Their needs are the same as refugees. The main difference between displaced people and refugees is that refugees have left their own countries.

One person out of every 150

people alive today is a refugee or displaced person. There are refugees living in every country in the world, but today most refugees live in the poorer countries of Africa or Asia. Most of the world's displaced people also live in the poor countries of Africa, Asia. or South America.

Everyday people run away from their homes because war puts their lives in danger.

In some countries, a person's political beliefs put them in danger. People may not be allowed to criticise their government in some countries. If they do so they may be arrested or killed. Refugees may escape from countries like Kenya, Syria or Burma because they belong to certain political parties.

In some countries, a person's

religion may put them in danger. The lives of some Christians, Baha'i and Jews are in danger in Iran.

People may be in danger in some countries, simply because they belong to a certain ethnic group. Albanian people are in danger in part of the Federal Republic of Yugoslavia called Kosova.

Sometimes, a person's chosen way of life puts them in danger. In Bhutan, laws have been passed that make a person wear a certain type of clothes. Those who do not obey this law may be sent to prison.

Dictionary

An ethnic group is a group of people who share the same culture and language.

A Kenyan refugee family in London. The father was in danger in Kenya because of his political beliefs

JON SPAULL

Information

Refugees around the world

Refugees in Europe
About 5 million refugees are living in western Europe. They have fled from many different countries.

Bosnia and Croatia
More than 3.5 million people fled from their homes between 1991 and 1995 during the fighting in Croatia and Bosnia. Today there are still 600,000 Bosnian refugees. Most of them live in Croatia and in Germany. Another 840,000 Bosnian people are homeless in Bosnia.

Federal Republic of Yugoslavia
In 1998 fighting between Serbs and Albanians started in Kosova, in the Federal Republic of Yugoslavia. Ordinary Albanian people who live in Kosova have run away from their homes. Over 450,000 people are refugees or displaced people.

Fighting in the Caucasus
Five wars are being fought in southern Russia, Armenia, Azerbaijan and Georgia. In this part of world, known as the Caucasus, there are 1,720,000 refugees and displaced people.

The Palestinians: refugees for 50 years
There are over 4,250,000 Palestinian refugees living in the Gaza Strip, the West Bank, Jordan, Syria and Lebanon. They fled their homes after Arab/Israeli wars in 1948/49, 1967, 1982 and after the Gulf War of 1991.

Kurdish refugees
Over 20 million Kurdish people live in the Middle East. In Turkey, Iran and Iraq, the Kurds have faced many dangers since the 1920s. Today there are over 400,000 Kurdish refugees in Europe and the Middle East. Another 1,100,000 Kurds have had their homes destroyed in Turkey and Iraq.

In danger in Colombia
Fighting in Colombia has caused over 1 million people to flee from their homes. Most of them have gone into hiding in other parts of the Colombia.

Afghan refugees
There has been a war in Afghanistan since 1979 and many refugees have fled from their homes. Today 1,400,000 Afghan refugees live in Iran and 1,200,000 Afghan refugees live in Pakistan. Another 300,000 Afghan people are displaced in their own country.

Sri Lankan Tamil refugees
Tamil people in Sri Lanka are an ethnic minority group. Some Tamils want an independent country and have been fighting for this. Ordinary people have been caught up in the war between Tamil fighters and the Sri Lankan army. Over 170,000 people are refugees in India. Other refuges have fled to European countries and Canada. Another 800,000 Tamils people have fled their homes but stayed in Sri Lanka.

Bhutan
Over 100,000 Nepali speaking people have fled from their homes in Bhutan and are now living as refugees in Nepal. They have fled from their homes after the Government of Bhutan took away their rights to live in their country and tried to force them to wear Bhutanese national costume.

Refugees in West Africa
War in Sierra Leone and Liberia has caused more than 1,775,000 million people to flee from their homes.

Angola
There has been war in Angola for many years. Today there are 220,000 Angolan refugees living in other African countries. Another 1,200,000 Angolan people are displaced in their own country.

Congo (formerly known as Zaire)
Over 200,000 refugees have fled to other countries in Africa and in Europe. They are escaping fighting. Some refugees from Congo-Zaire are also people who have opposed the government and who risk being arrested or killed for their political beliefs.

Fighting and danger in Sudan
There has been war in southern Sudan since the 1950s. Today the Sudanese government also imprisons those people who oppose it. As a result over

350,000 people have fled as refugees. Another four million people have fled from their homes and moved to another part of Sudan.

War in Somalia

Refugees have been fleeing fighting in Somalia since 1988. Today there are over 665,000 Somali refugees in Africa and Europe. Another 200,000 Somali people are displaced in their own country.

Going home to Eritrea

The war in Eritrea ended in 1991. But fighting had destroyed houses, roads and schools and it was very difficult for refugees to return home. Now Eritrean refugees are starting to return home from the Sudan. Another 320,000 refugees are still living in the Sudan.

The emergency in Rwanda and Burundi

In Rwanda and Burundi there has been conflict between Hutu and Tutsi people for many years. In June 1994, about 1,500,000 people, mostly Tutsi, were murdered in Rwanda. In Burundi, both Tutsi and Hutu people are being killed by racists. Today over 870,000 people have fled from their homes in Rwanda and Burundi and are refugees or displaced people.

Refugees have also fled from many other countries, including Algeria, Bangladesh, China (Tibet), Guatemala, India, Iraq, Iran, Kenya, Mali, Mauritania, Myanmar (Burma), and Western Sahara.

GUATEMALANS

COLOMBIANS

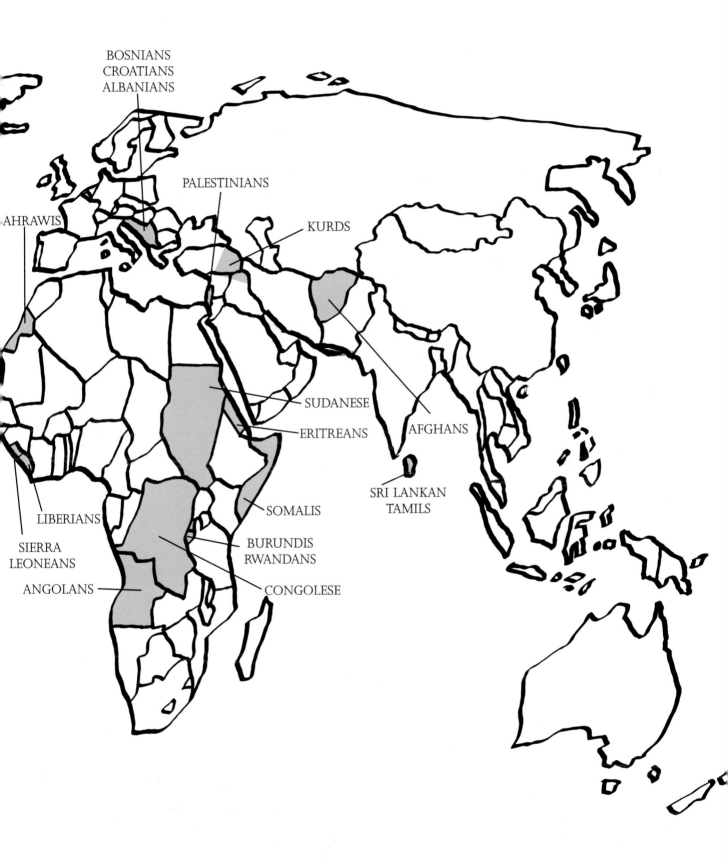

BOSNIANS
CROATIANS
ALBANIANS

PALESTINIANS

KURDS

AHRAWIS

SUDANESE

ERITREANS

AFGHANS

SRI LANKAN
TAMILS

SOMALIS

LIBERIANS

BURUNDIS
RWANDANS

SIERRA
LEONEANS

ANGOLANS

CONGOLESE

Activity

Word search

Hidden in the letters below are the names of ten countries or places from which refugees are fleeing. Can you find them?

```
E  B  O  P  S  Z  S  S  W  C  K  A  F  A  K  K
K  U  D  L  B  U  O  S  O  R  S  V  P  H  O  P
Z  R  V  L  O  M  D  L  P  G  C  A  L  S  V  U
T  U  S  P  A  M  O  A  H  M  R  M  O  H  F  Z
V  N  E  L  M  M  K  A  N  T  Q  V  S  J  O  C
G  N  I  A  B  P  N  J  H  G  A  R  Y  C  O  A
D  I  Y  I  L  I  A  E  N  T  S  K  U  S  Y  L
A  W  A  A  S  G  I  X  N  D  B  R  M  R  S  I
M  C  H  T  X  D  P  R  K  E  D  D  F  I  U  V
Y  F  A  R  X  K  P  R  O  T  N  G  T  L  Q  E
P  N  P  I  P  A  R  P  I  I  A  I  E  A  I  R
H  T  Q  R  L  Z  A  G  T  A  W  D  N  N  D  A
U  B  Q  A  Z  N  Z  I  Q  D  A  P  K  K  V  T
T  J  O  Q  J  X  E  B  T  A  C  H  A  A  S  E
G  U  M  Z  K  S  G  C  Y  T  R  V  L  N  Q  W
T  U  R  K  E  Y  B  B  Y  E  L  G  Y  E  N  P
```

Kurdish refugees in London at a self-help group   HOWARD DAVIES.

Answers:
SOMALIA
SRI LANKA
KOSOVA
IRAQ
AFGHANISTAN
BURUNDI
SUDAN
COLOMBIA
ALGERIA
TURKEY

16

Testimonies

Sado's story

Sado was eight years old when she fled from Somalia.

"I came back from Sunday school and I remember seeing that our living room as well as our kitchen had collapsed. Then I saw tanks in front of our house and they began firing. It was terrible.

We ran as fast as we could, my mother holding my hand. There was also Feriyo, my friend, as well as her granny who was running behind us because she could not catch up with us. She was old. President Siad Barré's picture was everywhere. I used not to look at him, but while we were running I saw a huge picture of him and I was scared.

Feriyo fell down while we were still running and there was this deafening noise. I let go of my mother's hand and ran back to help Feriyo but she wouldn't stand up. I shook her saying, "Feriyo, stand up." I begged her to stand but she wouldn't.

I have lots of friends here in my new school in London and they are all nice but I still remember Feriyo. She was so nice."

Manuel's story

Manuel has been a refugee twice. His mother is originally from Chile and worked with poor farmers in Chile and Argentina. Manuel's father is from Uruguay and is from a family of sugar cane workers. He was one of the founders of a political party called the National Liberation Movement of Uruguay. When Manuel's parents were working in Argentina, the Uruguayan police, with the agreement of the Argentinian government, came to arrest them.

"My mother was a teacher who worked with poor people. Mabel and Chacha were our neighbours when I was a baby. They were very poor but we were great friends. When my mum and dad were arrested, Chacha hid me from the soldiers and looked after me. Then my mum was allowed to have me in prison for eight months. She says that one morning, very early, the soldiers came with guns and took the mothers away in a lorry to another prison, leaving the babies behind. After ten days they took us to our mothers again. We were dirty and skinny because nobody had looked after us. All the other babies were crying and did not recognise their mothers, but she says I was quiet and smiled at her. The new prison was better at first because we were all together in a sort of dormitory, with 75 women and seven children. Some of the prisoners were teachers and they made a kind of nursery in the corner for us. But

things got worse and so my mother asked our neighbours Mabel and Chacha to look after me. Chacha told me that they loved me very much and still do. Sometimes they took me to visit my mother, and also my father in his prison far away. Then my mother said I would be safer with my Aunt Tere and I went to live in Brazil with her family.

We had a great time on the beach in Brazil. We were barefoot most of the time and just wore shorts. I used to go fishing with my uncle. I can remember very clearly that I caught a fish once. I loved it when my mum's letters came through with the coloured pictures. Auntie read them to me and my cousins. Then we went to Argentina. My aunt had to go to many offices and talk to a lot of people to get my mum free. She said I was good to be patient. The two of us were in a hotel and I felt very important. I was four years old then.

They took my mum straight from the prison to the airport. She says she did not know I would be there. When the soldiers took off the handcuffs she could hug me. She hadn't seen me for two years but she was smiling and happy. A year later my father came out of prison and joined us."

Elmer's story

Elmer is Colombian. He and his parents left their homes because they were threatened by soldiers.

"We couldn't go into town, we couldn't get our things from the house because the army would grab my mother, my grandfather and kill them. Since we had no change of clothes, we repaired the clothes of my brothers. Then where we were staying was bombed and we had to run away again.

It was raining and we only had a small tent. All the children went inside and the adults stayed outside. Again the soldiers came near and they threw grenades. These made a terrible noise and we all cried out of fear. Then the soldiers bombed us from helicopters. It was just like a Rambo movie."

A displaced Colombian boy

JON SPAULL

Renovat's story

Renovat is from Burundi. He is a Tutsi. Renovat and his family used to live in a village but now they live in a camp for displaced people in Burundi.

"In 1993 some of our neighbours started stealing our family's goats, cows and crops. One night people came with axes and knives, so we ran away with some other neighbours. My grandparents were so old they could not run and escape. They were killed and the houses were burned by people who were once my friends.

We arrived at the camp after running through the bush. Life in the camp is difficult. There is not enough water for drinking or washing. Nor enough soap, clothes, blankets or sleeping mats. We are only able to eat once a day. But my father is fortunate. He has been able to get some money by working in the office of the local vet.

Despite the dangers my father decided to return to our village to see if it was safe to go back with the whole family. He came back with the news that it was still too dangerous. But one of our neighbours had harvested our family's crops and was saving them for us so that we will have some seeds to plant. This kindness shows that not all our Hutu neighbours hate the Tutsi. Some are kind, but it is the politicians that are causing the problems."

Activity

Refugee children's stories

Time needed: one hour.
You will need to enlarge and duplicate the table below so that everyone has a copy. Children should read the four stories, individually or in small groups, and then fill in the table. After they have completed the table they can consider the questions.

Alternatively, the stories can be read to younger children and the table can be completed as a whole class activity.

Using an atlas or a globe find the countries where Sado, Manuel, Elmer and Renovat have lived. Write them down.

What do Sado, Manuel, Elmer and Renovat have in common?

	Sado	Manuel	Elmer	Renovat
What made them leave their homes?				
Were they living in a safe place now?				
What differences are there between their lives and yours?				
What similarities are there between their lives and yours?				

Chapter Two

Refugees throughout History

Throughout history people have been forced to flee from their homes and become refugees. During the last 500 years over one million refugees have arrived in the UK. Many of them have made enormous contributions to British life. This chapter examines refugees of the past and what can be learned from these events.

The starting point of this chapter is the child's immediate locality and history. Refugee movements throughout history and past refugee communities in the UK are then examined.

A Ukranian refugee boy enjoys his first meal in the UK, 1950

Activity

All about my neighbourhood

A local history project offers many opportunities to look at refugees' contributions to life in the UK. Children can make their own book about people who have moved into their neighbourhood, including refugees. Alternatively they can make a collage about refugees (and migrants) links with their neighbourhood.

Some of the information in Chapter Six **Thinking About How We Receive Refugees** can be used in this project.

Places to look for information

There are many places that children can gather information. They include

- the school library
- the local history section in the local library
- a local history society
- a local museum
- older members of your family
- a bookshop

Migration

Children can start by researching who has moved into their neighbourhood during the last 2,000 years. Their list may include Celts, Romans, Anglo-Saxons, Vikings, Normans, Huguenots, the Irish, Germans, Jews, Chinese, Indians, Italians, African-Caribbeans, West Africans and so on. Children may wish to examine the reasons that each group has moved into the neighbourhood.

Place names

A place name can indicate what groups of people have lived in the area. The class may be able to find examples of Celtic, Roman, Anglo-Saxon, Viking and Norman place names. A few street names indicate the nationality of a group of people that settled there, for example

- the Little Sanctuary (London) is a small street near

Westminster Abbey, where previously refugees sought safety.

◆ Jew Lane (Sheffield) was a street where Jewish people lived and worked.

◆ Petty France (London) was a place where Huguenot refugees settled.

Buildings

Buildings can give clues about groups of people who have moved into a neighbourhood. The Huguenots built their own churches and their homes had a distinct architectural style. Children can find out if there are any Huguenot buildings in their locality. Places of worship are also worth researching. When were Roman Catholic churches built in the neighbourhood? What groups form the congregation? Are there any synagogues in the locality? When were they built? Are there mosques, temples or gurudwaras? When were they built? A class visit to local places of worship may provide useful information.

Businesses and shops

Businesses and shops can give clues about recent local history. Children can research the restaurants and cafes of their neighbourhood. They can see if shops cater for the needs of certain communities. The travel agents and shops that offer cheap international telephone calls can also give clues about groups of people that live in the neighbourhood.

Famous inhabitants

Famous people from different parts of the world may have stayed or lived in the neighbourhood. A library, local history society or local museum is often a good place to find out about the neighbourhood's well-known past residents.

Oral history

Children can interview older members of their family about changes to their neighbourhood. The school may also wish to contact local community groups and invite members to the school to be interviewed by children.

Information

Refugees in religious books

Throughout history people have had to flee as refugees. Many religious books describe refugees' stories.

Jewish history

The early history of the Jewish people contains many stories of refugees. The Book of Exodus describes the escape of Jewish people from Egypt. There the Jewish people lived as slaves. Their life was hard and cruel. The Egyptians so hated the Jews that the Pharoah (king) ordered that all baby boys be killed. One child escaped because his mother hid him in a basket in the river. His name was Moses. It was Moses who led the Jews out of Egypt to the Land of Israel (then known as Canaan) in aound 1,250 BC. Every year at Pesach (the Passover Festival), Jewish people remember the journey out of Egypt.

In 722 BC the Land of Israel was attacked by the Assyrian army. Jewish people were taken into exile by the Assyrians. To the south, Jewish people lived fairly peacefully until 586 BC. Then the armies of Babylon (now in Iraq)

destroyed the Temple in Jerusalem. Some 10,000 Jewish families were taken into exile in Babylon. Today's Georgian, Kurdish, Iraqi and Iranian Jews are the descendants of Jewish people who stayed in Babylon.

Christian stories

Soon after his birth, Jesus, with Mary and Joseph, had to flee to Egypt. They fled because King Herod ordered that all baby boys under the age of two be killed. Herod had heard that a new 'King of the Jews' had been born and he did not want to lose his throne. Later, the early Christians were put in danger because of their religious beliefs. Early Christians faced danger both from Jews and from the Roman rulers.

The Journey of the Prophet Mohammed

The Prophet Mohammed was born in Mecca in 570. At this time most Arabic speaking people worshipped many Gods. Mohammed was a shepherd until the Angel Gabriel appeared to him and told him that there was only one God. Gabriel told Mohammed that he must found a new religion. But the prophet Mohammed's religious beliefs were not supported by most people who lived in Mecca. Mohammed was considered to be dangerous. He had to flee. In 622, the Prophet Mohmmed entered the city of Medina. Mohammed's journey from Mecca to Medina in known as the *Hegira*.

Activity

Refugee stories in Holy Books

You will need books of Bible stories and library readers about Judaism, Islam and Hinduism. Using the information provided children should research refugee stories in holy books such as the Bible, Koran and Ramayana. Children can write about

❧ the Prophet's Mohamed's journey from Mecca to Medina

❧ the story of Rama and Sita in the Ramayana

❧ the journey of Moses and the Jewish people out of the Land of Egypt

❧ the attack of the Land of Israel by the Assyrian army and the removal of Jewish people to exile in Assyria

❧ the destruction of the temple in Jerusalem by the armies of Babylon and the removal of 10,000 Jewish families to exile in Babylon

❧ the flight of the infant Jesus, Mary and Joseph to Egypt to escape the murder of all children under two years by King Herod.

Children can extend this work by making a strip cartoon to illustrate the story of Moses, or the flight of the infant Jesus. It is not advisable to draw the story of the Prophet Mohamed's journey to Medina as Islam forbids the use of pictures to illustrate religious stories.

Information

Refugees in British history 1100-1970

12th and 13th century

Jewish people were in danger in England. At this time the Church blamed the Jews for the death of Jesus Christ. In 1190 many Jews were killed in riots in London, Norwich, Lincoln and York. Other Jewish people fled as refugees. Later the Jews were expelled from England and only admitted back after 1665.

13th century

Small numbers of Armenian traders settled in Britain. They fled from Ottoman Turkey where their lives were in danger. They settled in Plymouth and London.

16th century

Roman Catholic refugees fled from England and Scotland during the 16th century. They were in danger because of their religious beliefs. One large group who fled were Roman Catholics who fled to Poland in the 16th century.

1572

French Protestants were in danger in France, because of their religious beliefs. On St Bartholemew's Day, 1572 many French Protestants were killed in riots. Others fled to Britain and settled in London and in the towns and cities of eastern England.

1560-1575

Dutch Protestants fled the Spanish Netherlands. There they were in danger because of their religious beliefs. Like the French Protestants, the Dutch Protestant refugees settled in London and in the towns of eastern England.

1665

Jewish people were allowed to settle in England, provided that they converted to Christianity. Those Jews who settled in England were mostly of Spanish and Portuguese origin, but living in the Netherlands. (Spanish Jews were expelled from their home country in 1492 and many settled in the Netherlands). Fish and chips were brought to this country by this group of Jewish people.

1685-1700

French Protestants were again in danger. Some of their churches were destroyed by Roman Catholic rioters and people were killed. Over 100,000 French Protestants fled to Britain and Ireland. The new refugees were known as Huguenots. Many Huguenots settled in London. Other towns with a Huguenot population included Bristol, Canterbury, Dover, Exeter, Ipswich, Norwich, Plymouth, Rye, Southampton, Derry and Dublin. The Huguenots brought new skills to Britain such as new ways of weaving silk.

1780-1900

There were many political changes in the governments of European countries. Small numbers of refugees fled from countries such as France, Italy, Germany, Poland and Austria. Their lives were in danger in their home countries because of their political beliefs.

1870-1914

Jewish people in eastern Europe faced many dangers at this time. In Russia, Poland and Romania Jewish people were killed in riots called pogroms. Jewish boys were also forced to join the Russian army. Jewish people also lived in a part of the Austro-Hungarian Empire called Galicia. Here they were very poor and at times did not have enough to eat. At the end of the 19th century over 200,000 eastern European Jews arrived in the UK. They settled in cities such as London, Leeds and Manchester.

1914-1918

Over 250,000 Belgian refugees fled to the UK, escaping the fighting of the First World War. Almost all of them returned home in 1918.

1933-1939

Some 56,000 refugees from Nazi Germany, Austria and Czechoslovakia fled to the UK. Most of them were Jewish. Among the refugees who came were 17 people who were later to win Nobel Prizes.

1937

Nearly 4,000 Basque refugee children arrived in the UK. They were fleeing from the fighting of the Spanish Civil War. They first stayed in a camp near Southampton. Most of the children returned home when the fighting stopped.

1939

Nearly 100,000 refugees from Belgium, France, the Netherlands, Denmark and Norway came to the UK, fleeing from the advancing army of Nazi Germany. Almost all of the refugees returned in 1945 at the end of the Second World War.

1939-1950

Some 250,000 Polish refugees settled in the UK. They arrived during the Second World War, or came in 1945 as part of a group of Polish soldiers who fought in the British army. Later other Polish refugees arrived from refugee camps in Europe, or fled from the new communist government in Poland.

1945-1960

Over 50,000 refugees from the Soviet Union, Romania and Czechoslovakia arrived in the UK. Some of them were living in refugee camps at the end of the Second World War and did not want to return to their home countries. Other refugees were political opponents of the new communist governments in eastern Europe.

1956

In November 1956 many Hungarian people decided that they wanted more freedom. They did not want to be ruled by a communist government. Hungarian people took to the streets. But the Red Army of the Soviet Union invaded and many people were killed in street fighting. Hungarian refugees fled their country. Over 17,000 Hungarian refugees arrived in the UK.

1968

In 1968 people in Czechoslovakia were given more freedom by a new communist government. But the governments of other eastern European countries did not like this. The armies of the Soviet Union and other eastern European countries invaded Czechoslovakia. Thousands of refugees fled. Nearly 5,000 refugees from Czechoslovakia settled in the UK.

1968-1970

Over 25,000 Irish people from Northern Ireland fled to the Republic of Ireland and to other parts of the UK. Many of those people who fled were living in areas where Roman Catholics and Protestants lived side-by-side. They received threats to their lives in order to get them to leave an area.

Polish refugee children in a refugee camp in Germany. These children later settled in the UK

BRITAINS FIRST REFUGEES

1.

THROUGHOUT HISTORY MANY DIFFERENT PEOPLE HAVE FLED TO ESCAPE PERSECUTION.
IN THE 1680's 100,000 HUGUENOT REFUGEES SETTLED IN BRITAIN.

2.

Arbour... Delahunt... Lefevre.... Bygott.... Coutauld...

THE HUGUENOTS GAVE THE WORD 'REFUGEE' TO THE ENGLISH LANGUAGE.

3.

DURING THE 18TH AND 19TH CENTURIES MANY WARS WERE FOUGHT IN EUROPE. IN FRANCE, POLAND AND OTHER COUNTRIES THERE WERE CHANGES OF GOVERNMENT. FOR MANY PEOPLE LIFE HAD BECOME DANGEROUS AND THEY HAD TO LEAVE THEIR HOMELANDS......

4.

POLITICAL EXILES LEFT FRANCE, GERMANY, AUSTRIA, ITALY, POLAND, AND RUSSIA, MANY OF THEM CAME TO BRITAIN.
THE BRITISH GOVERNMENT DID NOT FORMALLY WELCOME THESE REFUGEES, BUT THE POLICE DID NOT BOTHER THEM. THEY WERE ALLOWED TO TRAVEL AND LIVE WHERE THEY PLEASED.

5. LONDON BECAME KNOWN AS A PLACE WHERE REFUGEES COULD FIND SAFETY. IN THE 1850's ABOUT 4,000 REFUGEES WERE LIVING IN LONDON....

Karl Marx

Prince Metternich

Giuseppe Mazzini

6. BETWEEN 1880 AND 1914 ABOUT 120,000 EASTERN EUROPEANS JEWS SETTLED IN BRITAIN. THEY HAD LEFT THEIR HOMES IN THE RUSSIAN EMPIRE, RUMANIA AND AUSTRIAN GALICIA.

THE JEWISH PALE OF SETTLEMENT IN RUSSIA 1835-1917

7. THE JEWS WHO LEFT RUSSIA AND RUMANIA WERE REFUGEES. IN THESE COUNTRIES JEWS FACED THE VIOLENCE OF 'POGROMS'. POGROM IS THE RUSSIAN WORD FOR A RIOT.

YOUNG POGROM VICTIMS IN DNEPROPETROVSK IN THE UKRAINE

8.

JEWS FACED OTHER FORMS OF RELIGIOUS PERSECUTION IN RUSSIA. THEY FACED DISCRIMINATION IN EDUCATION, FORCED CONSCRIPTION INTO THE RUSSIAN ARMY, AND DISCRIMINATORY LAWS WHICH EXCLUDED THEM FROM CERTAIN JOBS AND FORCED THEM TO LIVE IN PARTICULAR PLACES.

9.

THE JEWISH REFUGEES WHO CAME TO BRITAIN WERE VERY POOR. ABOUT HALF OF THEM SETTLED IN WHITECHAPEL, THE POOREST PART OF LONDONS EAST END.

10.

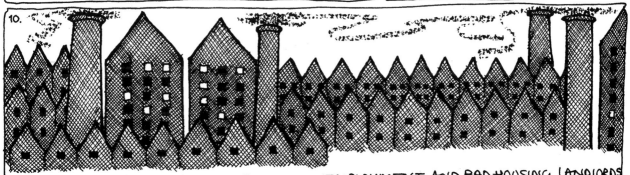

WHITECHAPEL WAS AN AREA OF HIGH UNEMPLOYMENT AND BAD HOUSING. LANDLORDS DID NOT REPAIR HOMES, MANY HOUSES WERE DESTROYED TO MAKE WAY FOR RAILWAYS AND OFFICES. SOME EAST ENDERS RESENTED THE JEWISH REFUGEES. THEY MADE THE MISTAKE OF THINKING THE REFUGEES WERE TAKING THEIR JOBS AND HOUSING.

31

11.

IMMIGRATION SOON BECAME A POLITICAL ISSUE. SOME M.P's, POOR EAST ENDERS AND RICHER JEWS OPPOSED THE UNLIMITED ENTRY OF POOR JEWISH REFUGEES FROM EASTERN EUROPE. POLITICIANS FELT THEY COULD WIN VOTES BY STOPPING EAST EUROPEAN JEWS ENTERING BRITAIN . . . .

12.

DURING THE YEARS 1900~1915 MAJOR GENERAL EVANS GORDON LED THE ANTI IMMIGRATION CAMPAIGN. HE ORGANIZED MEETINGS, MARCHES AND ALSO LEAFLETTING. HIS SUPPORTERS BROKE THE WINDOWS OF JEWISH HOMES AND CARRIED OUT VIOLENT ATTACKS...

13.

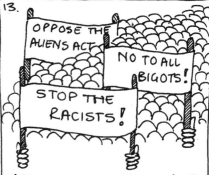

OPPOSE THE ALIENS ACT

NO TO ALL BIGOTS!

STOP THE RACISTS!

JEWISH EAST ENDERS AND SOME TRADE UNIONISTS AND POLITICIANS ORGANIZED THEIR OWN MEETINGS AND DEMONSTRATIONS TO OPPOSE MAJOR GENERAL EVANS GORDON AND HIS RACIST CAMPAIGN.

14.

HERE, HERE!!

GREAT IDEA!

ALIENS ACT OF 1905

MORE!

LOVE IT!

HOWEVER, AS A RESULT OF EVANS GORDONS CAMPAIGN THE BRITISH GOV'T PASSED THE ALIENS ACT IN 1905. THE ALIENS ACT COVERED ALL IMMIGRATION, INCLUDING ENTRY OF REFUGEES....

15.

TILBURY IMMIGRATION DESK

That's right! It's called a point of entry — but it's not so for everyone!

16.

THE ALIENS ACT OF 1905 EXCLUDED THE IMMIGRANT WHO WAS SICK AND THOSE WHO MIGHT NOT BE ABLE TO SUPPORT THEMSELVES.

IN 1906 ABOUT 4% OF JEWISH IMMIGRANTS WERE REFUSED ENTRY TO BRITAIN...

THE JEWISH CHRONICLE CARRIED THE FOLLOWING REPORT IN 1907....

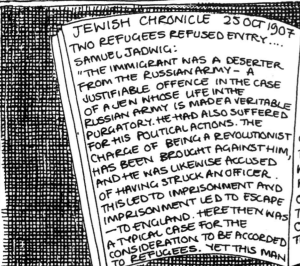

JEWISH CHRONICLE 25 OCT 1907
TWO REFUGEES REFUSED ENTRY....
SAMUEL JADWIG:
"THE IMMIGRANT WAS A DESERTER FROM THE RUSSIAN ARMY — A JUSTIFIABLE OFFENCE IN THE CASE OF A JEW WHOSE LIFE IN THE RUSSIAN ARMY IS MADE A VERITABLE PURGATORY. HE HAD ALSO SUFFERED FOR HIS POLITICAL ACTIONS. THE CHARGE OF BEING A REVOLUTIONIST HAS BEEN BROUGHT AGAINST HIM, AND HE WAS LIKEWISE ACCUSED OF HAVING STRUCK AN OFFICER. THIS LED TO IMPRISONMENT AND IMPRISONMENT LED TO ESCAPE — TO ENGLAND. HERE THEN WAS A TYPICAL CASE FOR THE CONSIDERATION TO BE ACCORDED TO REFUGEES. YET THIS MAN

JEWISH CHRONICLE 25 OCT 1907
WAS REJECTED. THE REASON FOR REJECTION OF JADNIG WAS THAT THE MAN WAS WITHOUT MEANS."
ITZIG FRIMSTEIN:
"ITZIG FRIMSTEIN ARRIVED IN LONDON FROM RUSSIA WITH HIS WIFE AND TWO CHILDREN. THEY CAME FROM A SMALL TOWN IN THE PODOLSKY GOVERNMENT WHERE THERE HAD BEEN THREATS AND WINDOW BREAKING. IN THEIR FEAR OF SOMETHING WORSE TO COME THEY RESOLVED TO LEAVE THE COUNTRY AND TO GO TO ENGLAND. THE ENTIRE FAMILY WAS EXCLUDED."

THE ALIENS ACT STATED THAT REFUGEES FLEEING PERSECUTION SHOULD BE ALLOWED INTO BRITAIN. BUT THERE IS EVIDENCE THAT MANY GENUINE REFUGEES WERE REFUSED ENTRY.

Activity

Time lines

Time needed: 45 minutes.

This activity aims to introduce children to the idea of time lines as being a way of recording historical events in chronological order.

You will need to copy the information sheet **Refugees in British History 1100-1970** and enlarge and copy of the worksheet below. The children should read the information sheet, then mark the point of arrival or departure on the time line in the correct place. The arrival of Belgian refugees has been marked as an example.

Refugee Timeline

European refugees arrive in the UK after fleeing the Nazis

Belgian refugees arrive in the UK

Basque refugee children arrive in the UK

Refugees flee from Northern Ireland

Refugees from eastern Europe arrive in the UK

French Protestants arrive in England and Ireland

Polish refugees arrive in the UK

Refugees from Czechoslovakia arrive in the UK

Jewish refugees flee England

Jewish refugees from eastern Europe arrive in the UK

Armenian refugees arrive in England

Hungarian refugees arrive in the UK

Refugees from Nazi Germany, Austria and Czechoslovakia arrive in the UK

Dutch Protestants arrive in England

Roman Catholic refugees flee England and Scotland

French Protestants arrive in England

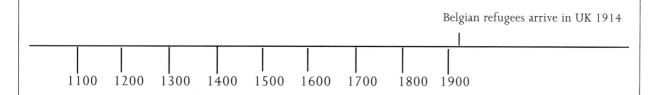

Belgian refugees arrive in UK 1914

1100   1200   1300   1400   1500   1600   1700   1800   1900

José's story

Jose Maria Villegas was born in Spain. He came to the UK as a refugee in 1937, as part of a group of 4,000 children.

"I was actually born in the south of Spain. But quite a lot of people used to go to Bilbao (in northern Spain) at the time, because there was work there. My father was a furniture maker. (He worked in Bilbao).

Just before the Spanish Civil War started my parents had gone back to southern Spain. I was left in Bilbao with my aunt and uncle. When the war started my parents were trapped in the south and we were trapped in the north.

Food became very scarce quite soon. By the time we came to England I don't think we had seen a white loaf for months. I remember we had to get up very early in the morning and queue up before the shops opened. You were supposed to have so many grammes of bread a day. At the beginning there was bread, and then they began to mix it with something else. In the end it was something black and we could not eat it.

By 1937 things in Bilbao were getting worse. First of all because the bombing was getting worse and then because food was getting worse and worse. They started to move children to France and Belgium.

We were going to this place that was called 'England', and probably we would stay there for a couple of months or something, and then come back.

I came with a friend, somebody who was living in the same block of flats as me. We came together and we spent three or four years in the same children's home. I remember the voyage. There were 4,000 of us on the boat, plus the crew and the people who were coming to help us. So, it was everybody sleeping everywhere, even in the life boats there were people sleeping. I was one of the lucky ones, I went straight to the hospital. We were sleeping in the hospital. I had a bed and we had someone who knew what to do when there were rough seas.

As the boat went out there were 4,000 kids and more or less everyone was sick and the poor sailors did not know what to do. Cleaning the place was almost impossible, as soon as they cleaned up, somebody else was sick."

Professor Ron Baker

Ron Baker was born Rudi Aschheim in Berlin in 1932. At the age of six his family sent him to Holland to escape the Nazis. He came to Britain in May 1940, on the last 'Kindertransporte' (the children's transport). He was fostered by the Bakers, a Jewish family from Salford, Lancashire. Ron Baker has worked as a psychiatric nurse, social worker and university teacher.

"I was born in Berlin in 1932, the year before Hitler came to power. I left Germany in 1938. Because I was so young, I don't have many memories of life in Berlin.

My mother sent my brother and me to Holland. My brother and I were separated when we got there and fostered by different families. We had very little contact over the next two years. I went to school in Holland and learnt to speak Dutch.

When Hitler invaded Holland I was put on the last boat that left for England. That was in May 1940. As the Nazis invaded Holland, Jewish refugee children were herded together. We were escorted through the German firing line in the docks. We were put on a boat. The memories of the boat were quite awful.

It was a boat of children, very few adults. There was a lot of fighting and bombing and we soon moved away from the port. As the boat steamed out, we passed through bombing for two or three hours. Why the boat did not sink I do not know. It took a week for the boat to get to Liverpool. We must have been a pathetic sight when we reached Liverpool.

We were housed in a church hall in Wigan for six months. We were looked after by volunteers. Although people were very kind, we couldn't actually talk, as language was a problem. Slowly, foster parents came to pick up the children, and one by one the hall emptied. I

remember being bundled into a car. I was picked up by this family called Baker. Overnight my name changed from Aschheim to Baker.

The next twelve months were difficult. I suffered nightmares and later the Bakers told me I sobbed myself to sleep for months. I was with the Bakers until 1947, when suddenly the Red Cross tracing service linked me with my mother who was still alive.

My mother escaped from Germany in 1941 and managed to get to Uruguay. She lived in dire poverty in Uruguay for five years. In 1947 she left Uruguay to go and live in Israel and on her way, came to see me.

The Bakers became very upset when they realised I had a mother. My mother stayed for three weeks. It was an odd time. To me she was a stranger. I was totally English. She went off to Israel. I did not see her again until 1954. My mother died in March 1988 in Israel. She was 86.

My father and brother perished. At the end of the war I knew they had died and I was told they were killed in Auschwitz.

My brother and a group of children were being trained as farmers to go to Palestine. When the Nazis invaded Holland seven of them tried to escape. They were caught by the Nazis, on the Belgian border, and were eventually sent to Auschwitz. A monument was put up to the children in the village in Holland where they had lived. I hope to visit this monument soon."

A Jewish refugee girl arriving by herself in the UK, 1938
WIENER LIBRARY

Karl Marx

Albert Einstein

Sun Yat Sen

Jesus Christ

Activity

Famous refugees

Time needed: one hour in a library for research.
Each child will need a copy of the line drawings and the short biographical details.

The people on all of these cards have had to become refugees at some time in their lives. Using biographical dictionaries or junior encyclopaedias, children should match the line drawings with the short biographical details. The drawings and biographical details can be used to make a poster or collage about famous refugees.

1879-1955. He was a German Jewish physicist. In 1933 he fled from Nazi Germany, moving first to the UK and then to the USA.

1866-1925. He was a Chinese political leader who fled from China in 1895. He lived in Japan, USA and Britain before returning to China in 1911.

1818-1883. He was a German philosopher and the founder of communism. His political beliefs meant that he was in danger in Germany and he fled to London in 1849.

He founded the Christian religion. As a baby he and his family had to flee from Israel to Egypt. His life was put in danger by King Herod who was killing all baby boys.

1891-1974. He was Emperor of Ethiopia. He had to flee to the UK twice in his life, the first time when the Italians invaded Ethiopia and then again in 1974 after his government was overthrown.

1935-. He is a Tibetan Buddhist leader. In 1959 he had to flee from Tibet after his country was invaded by China. He now lives as a refugee in India.

Dalai Lama

Sigmund Freud

Victor Hugo

Vladmimir Illich Ulyanov (Lenin)

Camille Pissaro

Rigoberta Menchu

1856-1939. He was a psychologist. Born in Vienna, he fled to London in 1938 after Austria became part of Nazi Germany.

1830-1903. He was a French painter. When he was 40 he had to flee to London to escape the violence and political changes in Paris.

1834-1890. He was an American Sioux chief who fought the US army in the Sioux War of 1876-77. After the war he had to escape to Canada.

1870-1924. He was a Russian communist and political leader. His political beliefs meant that he had to flee to Switzerland.

1802-1885. He was a French writer. His political beliefs meant that he had to flee France several times during his life.

1959-. She is Guatemalan and was born to a poor Quiche Indian family. Her father, mother and brother were killed because of her father's political beliefs. She fled to Mexico as a refugee and began work to help other Guatemalan refugees or those in danger in Guatemala. She wrote a book about her life and in 1992 won the Nobel Peace Prize.

Sitting Bull

Haile Selassie

Chapter Three
Escape from Danger

This chapter looks at what makes refugees leave their homes. It examines the dangers faced by Afghan, Sudanese and Roma refugees and by Albanian refugees from Kosova.

Through the use of activities, this chapter explores the causes of armed conflict and group persecution.

Bazihaziki a 14 year old refugee with Havu a two year old orphan. Bazihaziki found Havu by the side of the road when he and his sister were fleeing from Rwanda. Bazihaziki and his sister have been caring for Havu for one month, despite they themselves having been orphaned by the war in Rwanda   HOWARD DAVIES

Activity

Feeling scared

Time needed: one hour.
The activity looks at situations where children might feel scared and have to run away. You will need the children's paintings from the photopack. The children will also need paper and pens.

The class should be divided into groups of three or four. In the groups the children should write down times when they have felt scared. After this the children should write down times they have felt scared and have had to run away. This might, for example, have been times when they have been bullied. Younger children can draw pictures of times they felt scared.

The class should then come together. The children's experiences of feeling scared and having to run away should be compared.

Then the children should look at the paintings done by refugee children. The children should be asked what they see in the paintings. Then they can be asked what might have made the refugee children run away.

Fear and escape

The testimonies and information in this chapter can be used to stimulate creative work around the theme of fear and escape. Children can write their own imaginary stories about escaping as a refugee. They could also write a newspaper article about the danger face by people in places such as Afghanistan, Sudan, Kosova or the Czech Republic and Slovakia.

Children can also paint pictures about fear and escape, or use other media to illustrate these themes. The pictures below show one class art project about the fear and escape of one refugee boy.

The project was the story of Jediyon, an Eritrean refugee boy at Edgware School in London. After a journey that took them to the Sudan and then to Saudi Arabia, Jedyon arrive in London. Here he told his story to his English

teacher. Later, with the help of an artist and ten of his friends, the group illustrated his story, using paint, papier maché, calligraphy and other media. Jedyon's story was then published as a book called 'Eritrea to Edware' and the art has been displayed. Both the book and the display have helped raise awareness about the experiences of refugee children.

I was born in Asmara, Eritrea, on the 29-10-78. My Dad left me when I was three months old, he went to Sudan because there was a war and he may have had to join the army. After this I lived with my Mum. She always bought me sweets when I went shopping with her. One day, when I was about four years old, my father sent my Mum a letter. Now he was in Saudi Arabia. The letter said he wanted her to go to him there. I didn't get a visa, maybe because it was too much money, it costs about 12,000 Saudi rea. I remember my mum going to the airport, I went with her. I was crying when my mother left, I felt as if I would never see my mum again. My grandmother told me to stop crying, she gave me some money and a photograph of my mother. Then my grandma looked after me, My grandma was kind, she cooked me good food. She only ever hit me twice and that was for a good reason.

When my grandma was looking after me, we only stayed in my mum's house for another two weeks. Then we left because the house was taken back as my mum wasn't there any more. We went to my grandma's house, she lived in a village called Adicola. The village was very small it wasn't like Asmara. After about four weeks I had lots of friends, we played outside together. I went to my grandma's brother a lot of times. He had a big house and he was a very rich man. He even had a bar like an hotel. My grandmother had three children, they were called Musai, Adyam, and Sanayet. Musai a boy, Adyam and Sanayet were girls. One day when I was small I remember hearing my mother say that grandma had an older girl who had died. I went to school while I was living in that village. I learned to read, it was hard at first. In my second year I was top of the class, I was happy about that everyone was.

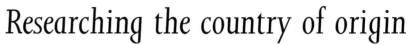

Activity

Researching the country of origin

Developing research skills is an essential part of the school curriculum. Children can find out more about countries of origin of refugees. They can collect information from library books and newspapers. They can also interview refugee students in their school, or visiting speakers.

Interviewing a visitor to the school is a skill. The class might like to use the following checklist so that they get the most out of their visitor.

Interview checklist
❯ Fix a date and time for the visitor to come to the class.
❯ Teacher should find out in advance about the visitor's background.
❯ The country of origin of the visitor and his/her background should be discussed with the children.
❯ Children should then write down a short list of questions to ask the visitor.
❯ When the visitor arrives in class the children should take turns to ask questions
❯ Record the answers on tape.
❯ A child should be given the task of thanking the visitor.

The information that the children find out can be displayed in different forms, including
❯ Radio drama
❯ Radio documentary
❯ A short fictional story
❯ A poem
❯ A factual article
❯ A newspaper article or newspaper spread
❯ A comic strip account
❯ A poster or painting
❯ A classroom display

Testimony

Wali's story

Wali is ten years old. He is an Afghan refugee. He now lives in London with his family.

"I was born in Afghanistan, in Kabul. Kabul is the capital city of Afghanistan. We lived in a brick house. We were not poor, but we were not rich. My father worked at the civic centre and my mother was a housewife.

When I was small I was quite happy. Life was very happy. Life was not hard and people were always kind to me. I went to school and I was in Class Six. My teacher was very kind to me. I always did my homework and I had many friends. After school we would go for a walk and play football together. Sometimes we would have a picnic.

Fighting started in Afghanistan. One night some men came to our house and took my father away and he was shot. Our life became very hard. There was fighting in other cities but the fighting started in Kabul in the summer of 1992. One morning at about four or five I was woken up by a noise. My mother and my family went into the corridors where there were no windows. The rockets came in fours. We stayed in the corridor for about an hour. Then it was a little bit quiet so we came out and my mother started to cook. The rockets stopped coming to Kabul, but not for other cities near us.

After this there were lots of soldiers walking about. Sometimes there were bad soldiers who went into houses and took things. All the schools were shut. I couldn't go to see my friends because it wasn't safe to go outside. The only time my mother went out was to get food. We were lucky because my uncle had a car and we could go quickly to the shops. After living like this for a week, my family decided we had to leave."

Information

Afghanistan

Capital Kabul
Population 22 million
Languages Pushtu, Dari (a form of Persian) and other languages.
Ethnic groups Many different peoples live in Afghanistan. The main groups are the Pushtun, who speak Pushtu, Tadzhiks, Uzbeks, Turkomen and Hazara.
Exports Most Afghan people work as farmers, growing wheat, fruit and vegetables. Some farmers also grow opium poppies which are used to make heroin and other illegal drugs.

Until very recently Afghanistan was ruled by tribal leaders. Afghanistan's present borders were drawn in 1893.

In **1973** the King of Afghanistan lost his throne. He was replaced by his cousin who made himself president. As time went by the new president tried to stop all opposition to his rule. Many leaders of political parties left Afghanistan as refugees at this time.

In **1978** the President was killed and a new communist government took over. It tried to improve the lives of poor people, but the changes it made were carried out too quickly for people to accept. Many people opposed the new government. In the countryside people started fighting the new government.

Afghan refugee boy at Hawaii camp, Pakistan   HOWARD DAVIES

Over 200,000 refugees fled from Afghanistan at this time.

In December **1979** soldiers from the Soviet Union invaded Afghanistan to help the Afghan government. The fighting soon grew much worse and many more people fled as refugees. Most of the refugees lived in camps in Iran and Pakistan and life is very hard for them.

In **1989** the soldiers from the Soviet Union left Afghanistan. But the fighting continued with different Afghan groups fighting each other. Kabul, the capital city, was destroyed in the fighting.

In **1995** a new group called the Taliban, took over many parts of Afghanistan. By 1998, the Taliban controlled most of the country. Afghan people were happy that there was less fighting, but many of them were unhappy with the way the Taliban ruled the country. The Taliban stop girls from attending school and do not allow women to work outside the home.

In **1998**, there were still 2,600,000 Afghan refugees living in Iran and Pakistan.

Activity

Learn to cook some Afghan food

Rice and meat dishes form the basis of most Afghan meals. One such dish is known as *Kabeli*. It is a rice dish with nuts, carrots and raisins and is named after Kabul, the capital city of Afghanistan and is often served at parties or on other special occasions.

Ingredients for four people
30g of almonds
30g of shelled pistachio nuts
50g of raisins
450g of basmati rice
450g of lamb or chicken
Two small carrots
One large onion
One teaspoon of tomato puree
One chicken stock cube
One teaspoon of ground cummin
One teaspoon of ground coriander
Half a teaspoon of ground cardamon
Half a teaspoon of cinnamon powder
Oil
Salt
Black pepper

1. Wash the rice under a cold tap until the water runs clear. Soak the rice in water for 30 minutes before cooking.

2. Cut the chicken or lamb into cubes.

3. Cut the carrots into long thin strips and chop the onions. Fry the onions and carrots in some oil for about three minutes. Then add the raisins and nuts and cook for another minute. Put on a plate for later.

Continued overleaf

4. Place the meat in the frying pan and cook with oil for about five minutes, stirring all the time. The place the meat in a casserole dish. Add 250ml of water, the tomato puree and the chicken stock cube. Cook in the oven at 200 C or gas mark five for about 45 minutes, until the meat is tender.

5. While the meat is cooking, cook the rice. Put the rice in a saucepan and cover it with hot water. Add more hot water so that the level of the water is equal to the level of the rice. Then boil the rice for about ten minutes until it is almost tender. Test it by biting a grain of rice. Be careful not to burn your mouth!

6. Take the meat out of the oven very carefully. Using a spoon, place the meat on a plate. Add the spices, pepper, salt, rice, carrots, onions, raisins and nuts to the gravy left in the casserole dish. Turn out the rice mixture on to a big serving plate. Make it look nice. Then place the cooked meat in the middle of the rice mixture. The Kabeli is ready to serve!

An Afghan fruit salad

Fruit and nuts grow well in Afghanistan. They are often dried and sold in the markets of small towns. They can be eaten as snacks or made into deserts such as this fruit salad. Try it after Kabeli.

Ingredients for four people
100g of peeled almonds
100g of shelled pistachio nuts
100g of rubbed walnuts
100g of dried apricots
100g of fresh chopped apricots,
or fruit such as apple or peaches
100g of raisins.

Mix all the ingredients together and cover with cold water. Leave in the fridge overnight and eat the next day.

Testimony

Deng Yai's story

Deng Yai is a Sudanese refugee who now works as a senior English teacher for the Refugee Council.

"I was born in South Sudan near a small town called Aweil, in a village called Konger. I am the third in my family. I used to have three brothers, three sisters, one half brother and two half sisters, but now we are only six. Four of my family died because of lack of medical care in our village.

I have not seen my family for 12 years. One of my greatest wishes is to see my family again.

I have no birthday! This is not a problem in southern Sudan but it is in the UK. Both of my parents could not read or write, nor could anyone else in our village. My parents remembered that I was born in a year of hunger. They said in that year people used to go to Aweil to buy food. So when I was older I asked people in Aweil what year that was and they said 1966. I did not have a month or day and my parents could not remember any more.

In 1980 I had to go to a doctor in Khartoum. I went with my uncle. The doctor needed to know my birthday. I told him it was in 1966 but I did not know anymore. So the doctor wrote 1st January 1966 on the form. That became my birthday. Later I went to another doctor and he wrote 1st January 1965 on my medical form. So I became one year older.

My parents are farmers. I stayed with them in the village until I was about seven years old. I remember many of the things we used to do when I was young. We used to go swimming and wrestle in the sand. Often we played a game called 'crocodile' when one of us would dive into the water and try to catch the others. Sometimes we would make animals, like cows, out of clay. These were our toys.

We used to go hunting and fishing, too. Sometimes a group of us would collect fruit near the village.

As my parents were farmers we had to help with the farm work. I had to look after the cows when I was young. During the rainy season we had to help with the crops or look after younger brothers and sisters.

When I was seven I went to school in Wau. It is a small city, the nearest city to Aweil. I was taken there by my uncle who wanted me to go to school. But he had to convince my parents first. It took about three days to convince my father that I should go to school. After school I went to the University of Juba, but I could not finish my studies because of the war. Students who opposed the government were in danger. I had to leave the university because of this.

Then I got a scholarship to the University of Cairo (Egypt). There I spent four years studying English language and literature. After this I taught for three years in Egypt and did some translation too. In Egypt I taught Sudanese refugee children as well as adults. I also taught refugees from other parts of Africa - I taught them English and Arabic from beginner to advanced level. We opened our own classes, it was very successful.

After Egypt I got a scholarship to study in the UK. I studied how to teach English as a Second Language. At this time I applied for refugee status in the UK, as I could not go back to the Sudan. When I finished my course I did some voluntary work teaching English and then I got a paid job as an English teacher at the Refugee Council.

The war still goes on in the Sudan. It started again in 1983. Before that there was war from the 1950s until 1972. I remember part of the first war as a child, but I am very glad that I did most of my education at a time of peace.

In the future I want to share some of my expertise as an English language teacher with other teachers in the Sudan. I would like to train head teachers. And I want to go back to the Sudan very much."

Information

Sudan

Capital Khartoum
Population 28 million, including four million internally displaced people.
Languages Arabic is the official language. Other languages include Beja, Nuer, Dinka and English
Ethnic groups Many different peoples live in the Sudan. Most people in northern Sudan are Arabs or Nubians. The people of southern Sudan are mostly black Africans. Many different ethnic groups live in southern Sudan, including the Dinka, Nuer, Shilluk, Azande and Bari.
Religion Part of the cause of the war in Sudan is religion. Most people who live in northern Sudan are Muslim. Most people in southern Sudan are Christians or follow traditional beliefs. Some Christians living in Sudan have been dismissed from their jobs, or imprisoned because of their religious beliefs.

Sudan was called Kush by the ancient Egyptians and Nubia by the Greeks. In ancient times many different peoples lived in Sudan. Most recently, in the 7th century Arab people moved to live in northern Sudan.

In the late 19th century Africa was colonised by European countries. The UK became interested in the Sudan. In **1889** a British and Egyptian army

Sudanese refugee boy collecting firewood in a camp in Uganda   UNHCR

defeated the Sudanese. The UK and Egypt then jointly ruled the Sudan. At this time northern and southern Sudan were ruled as two separate parts of the same country.

In **1956** Sudan became an independent country. But fighting had already begun. Some southern Sudanese people feared that they would be controlled by the north. They wanted an independent country for the southern Sudanese. During the war, the Sudanese government spent a lot of money on weapons and little on projects to help poor people.

The fighting lasted from **1956** until **1972**. It caused nearly one million people to become refugees.

In **1983** the fighting between the Sudanese army and groups of armed southern Sudanese began again. The fighting stopped farmers from planting their crops and in 1984, 1987, 1988, 1990 and 1993 there was famine in the Sudan.

By **1998** the fighting had caused over 350,000 Sudanese people to flee as refugees. Another 4 million Sudanese people were displaced in their own country. Another 2,600,000 people were hungry because no crops had been planted.

Information

The Sudanese boy's march

In 1988 thousands of Sudanese boys were seen walking towards Ethiopia. They were mostly between eight and 16 years old. Most of the boys had come from villages in the Bahr el Gazal region of Sudan. Here they had fled attacks by Sudanese government soldiers. But as well as looking for peace and safety, the boys wanted the chance to go to school. (Most schools in southern Sudan had been closed because of the fighting).

The boys walked nearly 450 kilometres to Panyido refugee camp in Ethiopia. It was a dangerous journey. Some of the boys were killed by wild animals on the way. Others had died of hunger and disease. To get into Ethiopia the boys had to cross a river and some of them drowned.

When the Sudanese boys arrived in Ethiopia they were tired and very hungry. But at Panyido camp they received the care that they needed: food, clean water and the education that they so wanted. Nearly 5,000 boys lived in dormitories at night and went to school in the day.

The refugee boys' peaceful life ended in 1991 when there was a change of government in Ethiopia. The Sudanese refugee children were not longer welcome in Ethiopia. They were told to leave and go back to the Sudan. For nearly a week the boys had to run from Panyido refugee camp. Many of them were drowned in a river. Others were attacked by the Sudanese army and air force who dropped bombs on the returning refugees.

The boys settled for a while in Pochala and Nasir, two towns in southern Sudan. But they had to flee again when fighting came near these towns. They travelled to Narus, another town in southern Sudan. But there was not much food here and many of the boys grew sick. The United Nations, who were responsible for looking after the boys, decided that they would be safer in Kenya. They crossed the Kenyan border in trucks. After three months in a temporary camp, the boys were moved to Kakuma camp in Kenya. They have lived there since then.

Kakuma refugee camp is a camp of children and young people. There are about 15,000 children in a camp of 30,000 people. Most of these children are boys aged 10-18 years.

Some of the younger children are cared for by Sudanese foster parents. Most of the older boys live in group houses. Five boys live and cook together. All the housework is shared. There are schools and training projects for the children.

But life in the camp is not easy. There are many problems facing the children and those who look after them. The children miss their parents. Many of the boys have seen terrible fighting and as a result have nightmares and find it difficult to cope.

Some of the boys in Kakuma camp have also been child soldiers in Sudan. Children as young as ten have been forced to fight in southern Sudan. Child soldiers find it particularly hard to adapt to a more peaceful life. Some of the child soldiers have returned to fight in Sudan.

Most of the boys and young men are also without their parents and family. They have lost people who can give them advice and support. As a result a very small number of the boys have turned to crime.
Now social workers are trying to help some of the refugee boys return to their home villages. But it is a big job as families have to be found before a young person can return.

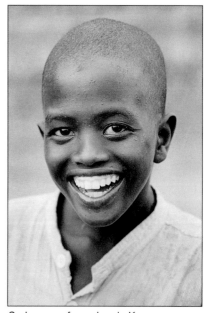

Sudanese refugee boy in Kenya   HOWARD DAVIES

Activity

Writing a newspaper article about the Sudanese boy's march

Time needed: one hour.
The aim of the activity is to get the class to write newspaper articles about the Sudanese boy's march.

The children will need paper and pens. They should also be provided with information material, including the information about the Sudanese boys march, an atlas and the sheet on the Sudan on page 51. The children might also like to use *One Day We Had to Run*, a book in which Sudanese refugee children tell their stories and *Refugee Children*, a free leaflet from UNHCR. (see further resources).

The children should imagine that they are foreign correspondents of a UK newspaper. They have been sent to Kenya to write an article about the Sudanese boys in Kakuma refugee camp in Kenya. The children can illustrate their articles.

Refugees flee because their lives are in danger. Many of them, like the Afghans and Sudanese may flee because of war. The next activities look at conflict as a cause of flight of refugees.

Activity

Conflict in my life

Time needed: 30 minutes.
This activity looks at everyday conflicts and their causes in children's lives. The children will need pens and paper; alternatively the activity can be carried out as a discussion exercise.

The class should be divided into pairs. The children should then be asked to list times in the last two days that they have got into 'conflicts' - arguments or fights with other people. After the children have done this, the class should come together. The teacher should then make a single list of some of the conflicts involving the children. Using the class list, the teacher should draw out some of the causes of the conflicts.

Activity

Different types of conflict

Time needed: one hour.
The activity aims to look at different types of conflict. You will need to photocopy the enclosed cards so that each group of children can see a set of cards.

The children should be divided into threes. In their groups they should look at each of the five cards and try and answer the following questions.
1. Who is involved in the conflict?
2. How did you think the conflict started?
3. What do you think that each side is feeling at the time?
4. What might happen next?
5. How might things be sorted out so that the conflict is stopped and everyone feels happy?

The activity can be followed up by starting to look at conflict resolution. This is followed up in Chapter Seven.

1

2

3

4

NO! YOU CANNOT MARRY JANE!

5

HOMES NOT MOTORWAYS

SAVE OUR HOMES

WE DON'T WANT TO LIVE ON THE HARDSHOULDER

Testimony

Rajmonda's story

Rajmonda is an Albanian from Kosova. She is now 20 years old.

"My father is a doctor. My mum is a nurse and they both worked in hospital. I've got two sisters and a brother. I had a very happy life with everything - nothing was missing.

I lived in Kosova. Here 90 per cent of the people are Albanians and 10 per cent are Serbians. Different groups. We had our own schools. We studied in Albanian. We had our own police, we had our own universities. Now they want us to study Serbian in school and do Albanian as a second language. Before it was the other way round, we did Serbian as a second language.

We were trying to get independence for Kosova. But bit by bit they were killing people. Then they started taking people out of jobs and filling them with Serbian people.

They closed our schools in Kosova. Always our dream was to go to university and study. Because they closed our schools we couldn't study. The police would not let us go to school normally, so we had secret schools. We went to schools in houses. People who left their houses to go as refugees to Germany or England, we used their houses as schools. They gave us permission to use their houses. We studied there, sitting on the floor, anywhere you can. Just a blackboard and that is it

I left my country two years ago. They threatened my brother when he was travelling to university. The police threatened him. They sent him a letter telling him to go to the army. In my country the army is compulsory and you have to go for a year. Whoever went from the Albanian people were sent straight to Bosnia, where war was."

Information

Albanian refugees

There are nearly six million people who speak Albanian in the southern Europe. Albanian is the national language of Albania where it is spoken by 3.5 million people. It is also spoken by 1.9 million Albanians who live in Kosova, part of the Federal Republic of Yugoslavia. Another 500,000 Albanian people live in Macedonia. Albanian speaking people also live in Greece and Italy.

Since 1992, Albanian refugees like Rajmonda have been fleeing from Kosova. Today there are 150,000 refugees from Kosova

Albanian refugees from Kosova at a shelter for homeless refugees in London
KAREN ROBINSON

living in other European countries. Another 300,000 Albanian people have fled from their homes but are still living in Kosova. A small number of Albanian speaking refugees have also fled from their homes in Albania and Macedonia.

In Kosova over 90 per cent of the people are Albanians. But Kosova is also important to the Serbian people. In the Middle Ages the first Serbian state was based in Kosova. It was the site of battle between the Serbs and Ottoman Turks. There are also

many historical Serbian churches in Kosova.

From 1945 until 1990 Kosova Albanians could attend Albanian speaking schools and universities.

But in 1990 all Albanian civil servants, doctors, nurses, teachers and lecturers were sacked by the government of Yugoslavia. Schools and hospitals were closed down. Albanian people decided to set up their own schools and hospitals, in houses, factories and restaurants.

Albanian people in Kosova have faced other dangers, too. Some have been imprisoned for their political beliefs or have been beaten by soldiers and the police. In 1998, fighting between the army of the Federal Republic of Yugoslavia and Albanian guerrillas grew worse. Ordinary people were caught up in the fighting and had to flee as refugees.

There are nearly 12,000 Albanian speaking refugees in the UK, mostly from Kosova. Many of them are young men aged 16-25 years, as they are at risk of arrest or being forced to join the Yugoslav Army.

Information

Teach yourself to count Albanian

 Four Katër

 Five Pesë

 Six Gjashtë

 Zero Zero

 Seven Shtatë

 One Një

 Eight Tetë

 Two Dy

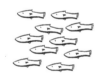 Nine Nentë

Three Tre

Ten Dhjetë

Albanian children at a school organised by their parents in Kosova MELANIE FRIEND PANOS

58

Testimony

Josef's story

Josef is a Roma refugee from Slovakia. He and his family fled to the UK in 1997. He now lives in Dover. But life has not been easy for him in his new home. The Roma have not been welcomed by many people who live in Dover.

"We had homes, cars and money but we had to flee from our country. Things are getting worse for us in Slovakia. The main problem is that we are being attacked by gangs of skinheads. In the last three years or so it has been getting worse and worse. Before 1989 the police helped us, now they are helping the skinheads.

In Slovakia the skinheads wear boots with black laces. If they have beaten up lots of Roma they wear white laces, like a medal. There are also cases of stealing where the Roma are blamed. Its not fair, we have not done it but they blame us.

I was beaten up one afternoon by a group of skinheads. I remember one behaving like the leader. He beat me very hard. A week later I saw the same man in police uniform. I went to the police station and told them it was one of their officers. They did not investigate. I wrote a letter to them asking why not? Then the next that happened was that the police called me into the police station and questioned me about different crimes.

I was beaten at the police station and I fell against a window and cut myself. Then they hit me with a chair. They told me that if I kept quiet about what I had done, they would let me off.

The situation for Roma is getting worse. We want action to change it."

Information

Roma in Europe

About 10 million people identify themselves as Gypsies in Europe. There are other Gypsies communities living in countries like the USA, Australia, Turkey and South Africa. European Gypsies had their origins in India. The first records of Gypsies arriving in Turkey and Greece date back to about 1000 AD.

The Gypsies fall into two groups. **Eastern Roma** live in eastern European countries like Hungary, Poland and Romania. Their home language is usually a dialect of Romanes, a language most closely related to Indian languages such as Hindi, Punjabi, Bengali or Gujerati.

Northern Gypsies live in northern and western Europe. They include the Sinti (German Gypsies), the Kalé and English Romanichal Gypsies. The Romanes language they speak is slightly different from that spoken by Eastern Roma. The first records of Gypsy people living in the UK go back to 1430. In 1530, the law was changed in England and being a foreign Gypsy became an offence punishable by death.

There are about 105,000 Kalé and Romanichal Gypsies living in the UK. In the last five years they have been joined by refugee Roma from Bosnia, Poland, the Czech Republic, Slovakia and Romania.

Bosnia About 250 Bosnian Roma refugees are now living in the UK. Most of them are living in London, Derby and Edinburgh. They came to the UK between 1993-1995 to escape the fighting in Bosnia.

The Czech Republic Here Roma have been victims of violent attacks for hundreds of years. In 1918 the area that is now the Czech Republic became a part of the new country of Czechoslovakia. Czech Roma were encouraged to live in settled homes. Czech Roma were also forced to carry special identity cards and were not allowed to enter certain areas.

In 1938, Nazi Germany invaded Czechoslovakia. Western Czechoslovakia was directly ruled by Nazi Germany. Between 1938 and 1945 over 10,000 Czech Roma were murdered by the Nazis.

After the Second World War the government of Czechoslovakia moved Roma from Slovakia westwards into the country that is now the Czech Republic. All Roma were forced to live in settled homes. The Czech Republic became an independent country in 1993. Most of the Roma living in the new country had originally come from Slovakia in the 1940s. Now many Roma have problems to get Czech passports.

Since 1993 violence against the Czech Roma has increased again. Gangs of skinheads attack Roma adults and children. The police have not tried to stop the skinheads and often refuse to investigate violent attacks on Roma.

Roma refugees started arriving in the UK in 1996. Now about 600 Czech Roma live here. Sadly, they have not always been made to feel welcome in their new homes.

Poland Roma have been the victims of violent attacks for hundreds of years. Between 1939-1945 over 35,000 Polish Roma were murdered by the Nazis who occupied Poland. Later, after Poland became a communist country, the Roma were forbidden to travel and forced to settle down in towns and villages. Since 1990, there have been more violent attacks on Polish Roma. The Polish police have refused to protect Roma and children are regularly bullied at school.

Polish Roma refugees starting arriving in the UK in 1994. Today there are over 2,500 Polish Roma living in the UK.

Slovakia Roma have been victims of violent attacks for hundreds of years. By the end of the 19th century almost all Slovakian Roma had given up the nomadic way of life. They lived in their own small villages and worked as blacksmiths, builders and musicians. In 1918 Slovakia became a part of the new country of Czechoslovakia.

In 1938, Nazi Germany invaded

A Bosnian Roma woman and her child at a reception centre for refugees in Derby HOWARD DAVIES

Slovakian Roma refugees started arriving in the UK in 1996. Now about 1,000 Slovakian Roma live here. They have not always been made to feel welcome in their new homes.

Romania Roma have been the victims of violent attacks for hundreds of years. Between 1939-1945 over 36,000 Romanian Roma were murdered by the Nazis. Later, after Romania became a communist country, the Roma were forbidden to travel and forced to settle down in towns and villages. Since 1990, there have been more violent attacks on Romanian Roma, with over 30 Roma killed. Roma children are regularly bullied at school.

In 1998 about 500 Romanian Roma came to the UK as refugees.

Gypsy Populations in European countries

Albania	95,000
Bosnia	45,000
Bulgaria	750,000
Czech Republic	275,000
France	310,000
Germany	120,000
Greece	180,000
Hungary	575,000
Italy	100,000
Macedonia	240,000
Poland	55,000
Portugal	45,000
Romania	2,100,000
Russia	230,000
Slovakia	500,000
Spain	725,000
Turkey	400,000
Ukraine	55,000
UK	105,000
Federal Republic of Yugoslavia	425,000

Source: Donald Kenrick: An historical dictionary of the Gypsy people.

Czechoslovakia. Between 1938 and 1945 1,000 Slovakian Roma were murdered. Roma were also sent to work camps, and stopped from using parks, cafes and public transport.

After the Second World War the government of Czechoslovakia moved Roma from Slovakia westwards into the country that is now the Czech Republic. Slovakia became an independent country in 1993. Since then

violence against the Slovak Roma has increased. Gangs of skinheads attack Roma adults and children. For example, in 1996 a gang of skinheads attacked a group of five Roma children from a special school. The children were travelling to see a hockey match. At least ten Roma have died as a result of violent attacks by skinheads. The police have not tried to stop the skinheads and often refused to investigate violent attacks on Roma.

Activity

Comparing Romanes with Indian languages

Time needed: 30 minutes.

The class will need access to a child or adult who speaks a language of the Indian sub-continent such as Urdu, Hindi, Gujerati, Punjabi or Bengali.

The activity should be introduced by the teacher. Romanes is most closely related to languages spoken in India, although the different dialects contain many words borrowed from the countries through which Gypsies have travelled. Romanes has also given words to European languages such as the English word pal, from the Romanes word *phral*, meaning brother.

The class should be given the numbers one to five in the dialect of Romanes spoken in Romania. Using the child or adult speaker of an Indian language, the Romanes words should be compared with the words from the Indian languages.

Romanian Romanes

1	Ek
2	Dui
3	Trin
4	Chtar
5	Pansh

Activity

Painting caravan motifs

The activity aims to get children to paint horse drawn caravan motifs used by Gypsies in different parts of Europe. The activity could be incorporated into work on migration or journeys. Children will need paper, pencils and paints. The illustration of the caravan and motifs can be copies from below. Pictures of horse drawn caravans and painted vehicle drawn caravans can be shown to the children. The activity could be extended by getting children to make their own Gypsy caravans.

The activity can be introduced by background work on European Gypsies and Travellers. From the 1830s until the 1960s Gypsies who still travelled used horse drawn caravans. The Romanes word for the caravan is *vardo*. It is thought that this word is of Ossetian origin and introduced to the Romanes language by Roma who travelled through the Caucasus. (Ossetian is a language spoken in Georgia and southern Russia).

The horse drawn caravans were converted from farmers carts. In 19th century Poland many richer Roma families owned a tent, a horse drawn caravan and a house that they used in the winter.

The caravans were decorated using carvings and paintings. Richer families had caravans that were more elaborately decorated. Different motifs were used in different European countries. Many of the patterns used were taken from popular patterns in the host society.

Caravan motifs used by Polish Roma include

Scrolls

Border patterns

Flowers such as tulips and lilies often painted in red and green.

Birds such as hens and doves.

Mythical animals such as griffins and dragons.

Activity

A refugee because I am different

Time needed: one hour.

You will need coloured stickers, chalk, marker pens and paper. The activity is best carried out in a large room with a smaller room attached, or a room and the playground. Two adults are needed to help with this activity.

The activity aims to help children think about some of the stages that led up to the persecution of political, religious or ethnic groups. Refugee may flee because their membership of a political party or their religious group puts them in danger, or because they face racial violence. For example, Albanian and Roma refugees have fled because they are in danger because of the ethnic group to which they belong.

But the present dangers facing Albanian and Roma refugees have not happened suddenly. There have been many stages leading up to the present, namely

1. Newspapers, politicians and ordinary people start talking about the persecuted group as being different from other people. A stereotype arises.

2. The persecuted group experiences discrimination in their everyday lives.

3. The persecuted group loses some of its legal rights.

4. The persecuted group is isolated from the rest of society.

5. Ordinary people cease to meet the persecuted group, and stop seeing them as human beings just like themselves.

6. There is an event that triggers violence against the persecuted group. This event gives the excuse to carry out violent attacks on the persecuted group. Those carrying out the violent attacks believe that they are right in their actions.

The teacher will need to introduce the activity and explain that the different treatment of groups of people can lead to a group of people facing violence. The activity will look at the dangers of treating groups of people differently.

The class should be divided and about one third of the children should be given coloured stickers. This group should be sent to another room. They are the 'outsiders'.

The rest of the children are 'insiders'. Sit with them and tell them that they are going to work out some rules for breaktime in schools. They will be able to make up five rules that govern the lives of insiders and outsiders. Any rule that gets a majority vote will be passed.

The rules could include:
➤ outsiders may not enter chalk circles unless invited;
➤ outsiders may only use toilets marked with a sticker.

After five rules have been decided they should be written on a large sheet of paper. The outsiders should then be invited back into the room. They should be told that it is ordinary breaktime, but they must also follow the rules decided by the insiders.

After ten minutes of the 'break' stop the simulation. The whole class should sit down and discuss the following points.

1. Did the children think the rules were fair?

2. What was the worst thing about being an outsider?

3. Where their any disadvantages about being an insider?

4. Did any of the outsiders try and do things that were forbidden to them? If so, how did the insiders react?

5. What did the insiders feel about the outsiders?

6. In the real world, how do you think that the outsiders might react? What do you think might happen in a country where there were 'outsiders'?

Chapter Four

The Journey to Safety

Many refugees who leave their homes have difficult and dangerous journeys. This chapter looks at the flight of refugees.

Vietnamese refugees flee by boat, 1989   UNHCR

Activity

What would you take and what would you leave behind?

Time needed: about 45 minutes.

Each child will need a copy of the graphic below and paper and pens.

The activity looks at what refugees might take and leave in their journey to safety. Introduce the activity by explaining that sometimes refugees have to leave their homes very quickly. Often refugees may not know where they are going and how long they will be away.

Pupils should imagine that they are in danger and that they have decided to flee. They do not know where they are going. They have 15 minutes to pack ten items in a small bag.

Each pupil should draw what they would take with them. After they have done this, the class can make a list of things that they value that they would have to leave behind. They should include non-material things, like friends, in their list.

The class lists can be compared and used to introduce work on the flight of refugees.

Testimony

Arjun's journey to safety

Arjun is a Tamil boy from Sri Lanka. At the age of six years Arjun and his mother and sisters fled from his home in Jaffna to escape fighting. It took the family three years to reach London and be reunited with Arjun's father who had left Sri Lanka before them. Like many refugees, Arjun's family had to pay money to agents to arrange their escape.

"We drove from Jaffna to Colombo by car and then took a plane to Singapore. We arrived in Singapore and stayed there for one week. It wasn't only us, there were plenty of people. They wanted to go to Germany and all different countries. They all lived in our hotel.

We stayed in our hotel for one week. The agents arranged all that. My dad gave money to them. And they gave us food and stuff.

And then we arrived in Bombay. From there I think it was Africa. And we stayed for two years because we had all these problems with passports and everything. The agents were messing us around and they lied to us, so we stayed there for two years. We stayed in a big house and we had to cook. We had no money and sometimes my Dad sent money to us.

Two men died in the house in Africa. They got sick with malaria, many people get sick there. All sorts of people came to the house, Sri Lankans to go to Germany, to Britain, to France and other places. Mum was angry with the agents because we were going to come to

Britain straight away from Colombo, but the agents made us stay in Africa for a long time.

There were six or seven rooms upstairs and downstairs in the house. Downstairs it was a big place and we could play there. I got to know some children because I stayed for two years and I got some friends. But I couldn't go to school.

Then I came to Holland and from Holland I came to Germany, Germany to France and it's a long story! This was all because of the agents as well. We spent a lot of money because of the agents.

I stayed in Germany for six months. We stayed with Auntie which was nice. From Germany I went to France in my uncle's car. Then we stayed in my uncle's house in France for about a week. We left France in my uncle's car and went to Dover. I didn't have a passport of my own, so I had to dress up as a girl! I had to dress up as a girl so when they asked for a passport we showed a girl's passport and we came through. I was wearing a hat. My sisters, they were laughing at me.

My Dad was in Britain, so that's why we came to Britain you see. He was over here before us and had lived in London for about six years.

We arrived in the morning about six. It was a Sunday. My dad, he was at home. He was different from before. He was very different and felt like a stranger to me.

It took two or three years to reach England. That is why I was late starting my education. It was hard on me at school. I was in Year Two in Jaffna and I was in Year Five in London.

I don't think about all of this anymore, but if I do, it's really strange and horrible."

Information

Sri Lanka

Capital Colombo
Population 17 million
Languages Sinhala and Tamil
Ethnic groups Sinhalese (74 per cent), Tamils (18 per cent), Muslims (7 per cent) and the descendants of Portuguese and Dutch settlers
Main exports tea, rubber, gems and clothing.

Fighting in Sri Lanka has caused over 450,000 Tamil people to flee as refugees to India, Europe and North America. Another 800,000 Tamil people have been made homeless in their own country.

Sinhalese and Tamil people have lived in Sri Lanka since the **5th century BC**. More recently

Ceylon (as Sri Lanka was known before 1972) was colonised by the Portuguese, Dutch and then the British. In the 19th century, the British Government bought more Tamil people to work on coffee and tea plantations in central Ceylon.

In **1948** Ceylon became an independent country. At this time, many Tamil people were worried about their future in a country in which they would be a minority. Their worries proved right. Between **1948** and **1958** many Tamil people lost the right to vote in Sri Lanka. Tamil civil servants also lost their jobs because Sinhala replaced English as the language of the Government. (Many Tamil people did not speak and write fluent Sinhala). In 1958 over 1,000 Tamil people were killed in riots.

By **1975** some young Tamils had had enough. They wanted an independent country for Tamil people. So they formed an organisation to fight for an independent country. By **1983** there is civil war in northern and eastern Sri Lanka. The fighting continues to the present day.

There are 33,000 Tamil refugees living in the UK. On Saturdays, many young Tamils attend mother tongue schools where they learn the Tamil language, music and dance.

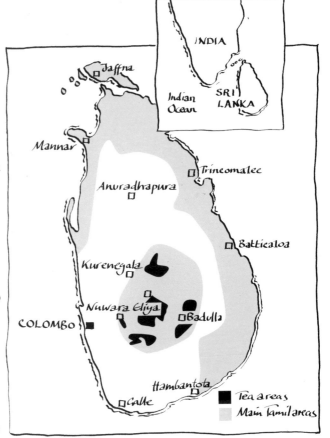

Tea areas
Main Tamil areas

Tamil refugees at a music class run by a refugee self-help group, UK   HOWARD DAVIES

The old men and the elephant

A Tamil folk story

Once upon a time there were six old men. They were neighbours in a small town. Old age had made the men blind.

One day an elephant was brought to the town. Everyone was very excited and all the people wanted to see the huge beast. The six old men wanted to see the elephant too, but how could they?

"I know," said the first old man. "We will go and feel it."

"That is a good idea," said the others. "Then we will know what the elephant is like."

So the old men set off to the town square to meet the elephant.

The first old man moved close to the elephant. He touched the elephant's big flat ear and felt it move back and forth. "The elephant is like a fan," said the first old man.

The second old man put his hands on the elephant's legs. "He is like a tree," said the old man.

The third old man was touching the elephant's tail. "You are both wrong," he shouted. "The elephant is like a rope."

The fourth old man reached up and touched the elephant's sharp tusks. "No, no," he cried. "The elephant is like a spear."

The fifth old man leaned back against the elephant's side. "I disagree," he said. "The elephant is like a high wall."

The sixth old man held on to the elephant's trunk. "I am right and you are all wrong," he said. "The elephant is like a snake."

"No, no, a fan."

"A tree."

"A rope."

"A spear."

"A wall."

"A snake."

With this the old men began to shout at each other. The elephant, an animal who does not like loud voices, walked away. The old men never did find out what the elephant was really like. Which all goes to show that if you do not listen to your friends, you will miss out on many things.

Testimony

Feysal's story

Feysal is from Somalia. He now lives in London. Like many refugee families, Feysal's family was split up when they left Somalia.

"When I was 13 years old we left Somalia to go to Kenya. My three big brothers were missing because of the fighting and my Dad stayed in Somalia to look for them. I left with my mum and the rest of the family. We saw my uncle and he had a boat so he took us to Kenya. My uncle had some friends in Kenya and we stayed with them. In Kenya we had to sell our watches to make money to live. After three months my Mum borrowed some money from my uncle and we came to England.

My Dad found two of my brothers and went with them to Saudi Arabia. My other brother managed to get out of Somalia to Yemen.

When I first saw England I felt free and safe. I felt like I was in a big air conditioned room because I felt cold.

I didn't speak any English and felt strange because I didn't know where I was and I didn't have any friends. After a few weeks I made some friends by going to the local park. Then we got a house and I started school. After a few months we changed houses and I went to another school. Eventually all my family met up in England apart from my older brother in Yemen who went to Holland."

Somali nomad boy paints Koranic verses on a board   HAMISH WILSON

Information

Somalia and
the Republic of
Somaliland

Capital Mogadishu. The main
city in the Republic of
Somalialand is Hargeysa.
Population 7 million
Languages Somali, Brava. Arabic
is also widely understood.
Ethnic groups Most people are
Somali. There is a minority
group called the Bravanese who
live in the towns of southern
Somalia. At home they speak a
language called Brava.
Religion Most people are Sunni
Muslims
Main exports Livestock to
Saudi Arabia.

Archaeologists believe that the
first Somali people settled in
East Africa about **2000 BC**. The
ancient Egyptians called Somalia
'the Land of Punt' meaning the
land of frankincense. Later Arab
traders settled in towns along
the Red Sea coast. Around **900
AD** Islam became the religion
of most Somalis.

In the **19th century** Somalia
was colonised by the British
and Italians. Somali sailors
joined the British navy, and later
settled in the UK. Somalis have
lived in places like London,
Cardiff and Liverpool since the
early years of the 20th century.

Somalia became an independent
country in **1960**, after British
Somaliland united with Italian
Somaliland.

In **1983**, guerrilla fighters who

Somali refugees at a clinic in a refugee
camp in Ethiopia   UNHCR

opposed the Somali government,
began fighting. The civil war got
worse in **1988** with the Somali
government bombing northern
towns like Hargeysa. Thousands
of people fled as refugees from
the fighting at this time. Some
Somali refugees settled in
Britain, joining relatives who
already lived here.

In **1991** the fighting caused the
Somali government to collapse,
and the President fled the
country. At the same time
northern Somalia declared itself
to be an independent country.
Since 1991, there has been peace
in northern Somalia (now the
Republic of Somaliland) but
fighting has continued in the
south. Refugees have continued
to flee from the fighting, leaving
for Kenya, Ethiopia, Yemen,
European countries and North
America.

Over 70,000 Somali refugees
now live in the UK.

Information

Somali nomads

Nomads are people who move with their animals in search of water and food. For as long as Somali people have lived in east Africa they have been nomadic farmers. Today about 40 per cent of Somalis are still nomads. Many Somalis who lives in the UK have relatives who are nomads.

The land

Most Somali nomads live in northern and central Somalia. This area is semi-desert and the land is too dry to grown crops. Nomadic farming is a very good way of using poor, dry land. Nomads also take great care of the land to ensure that it will provide for their grandchildren and great grandchildren, as well as other nomads.

Somali nomads   FIONA MACINTOSH

Animals

Camels are the most important possession of Somali nomads. They are called the ships of the desert because they carry goods and people. The camel's milk is drunk or made into butter and cheese. The camel's meat can be eaten or sold and its skin is made into leather. Somali nomads may also own cattle, goats and sheep.

The nomadic family

Somali nomads usually travel in a family group called a 'reer'. Grandparents, parents, children, uncles, aunts and cousins all move together. If food or water is short, the reer may sometimes split up and search for better food and water.

Moving

Somali nomads do not move without a plan. They know the times when rain is expected and know which places will have good grass for their animals. Most nomads follow a similar pattern of movement from year to year.

When the time comes to move, the reer packs up its possessions. Most important is the aqal, the portable house in which Somali nomads live. The house is made of curved branches, poles, leather skins and grass mats. Many nomads have also bought plastic sheets to make their aqals more waterproof. Grass mats form a floor inside the aqal.

The aqal and all the reer's possessions are loaded on to camels. The other animals are then collected. The family then walk alongside their animals in the journey to a new campsite.

The new camp

When the family arrive at the new campsite, they must put up the aqals and make pens for the animals. Building the aqals is usually the job for women and girls. First they put up the frame of curved branches. The mats, skins and plastic sheet cover the frame. Men and boys usually build pens for the animals.

A typical day

A nomad's day starts very early, when the sun rises. After washing and breakfast, some of the men and boys collect the animals from their pens and take them to eat and drink water.

During the day women and girls are also busy cooking and looking after small children. Milk is made into butter. Food is cooked for the whole day. If there is time, the women may weave grass mats.

Some of the family may go into towns to sell meat, milk and leather and buy oil, salt and other items that they might need.

More and more children from nomadic families are able to attend schools. Even if the children do not go to school they will have time off from work and play, to sit with the religious teacher. Almost all Somalis are Muslim. Somali children, in towns and in the countryside attend religious schools called madrassah. In the madrassah the children are taught Arabic and the teachings of the Koran.

In the evening everyone returns to the camp. Everyone has an evening meal. After they have finished eating, people sit around and talk. Most nomads now have radios and they may listen to them at night. Sometimes adults tell stories and poems to the children and to each other. Somalia is famous for its many folk stories and poems.

Activity

The journey to safety game

Time needed: about 45 minutes.

This game aims to highlight the difficulties faced by refugees in making their journey to safety. It follows the story of four young refugees who flee from their homes in Somalia.

The teacher/group leader will need to enlarge and photocopy the game board (enclosed with the book), role cards and chance cards. The sets of role cards and chance cards should be cut up. Each group of four players should have a game board, set of role cards and chance cards, and a dice. Every player should have a counter, pen and small piece of paper.

The board should be set out and the chance cards placed in alphabetical order on the board.

The class should be divided into groups of four. Each member of the group will take on a role of one of the refugees.

The game starts with all the players making a list of ten things that they would take with them on their journey. They should be items that a person can easily carry.

Participants need to shake a 'six' to start. When children land on a chance card square they will need to pick up the relevant card. The card should be read out to the group.

At the end of the game, the class should think about the discussion points.

Discussion points

❧ What was the most dangerous part of your journey?

❧ What was the least dangerous part?

❧ What did you learn from the game about the experiences of refugees?

Dictionary

Red Cross Messages The Red Cross runs a service called the Red Cross Family Message Service. This is for people who have relatives living in places where there is a war and where normal post and telephone services do not work. If you want to send a family message, you go to a Red Cross office and write your message on a special form. The message is then sent to the Red Cross office nearest to where your relatives are living. Red Cross workers take the message. Often people who have relatives who live in refugee camps will use Red Cross Family Message Service.

Role Card

Hassan aged 12 years, brother of Amina. Hassan and Amina are friends with Aysha and Mohammed, who also live in their street. Hassan has relatives in the next town. Like many Somalis, Hassan also has relatives who live in the UK.

Role Card

Amina aged 10 years, sister of Hassan. Hassan and Amina are friends with Aysha and Mohammed, who also live in their street. Amina has relatives who live in the next town. Like many Somalis, Amina also has relatives who live in the UK.

Role Card

Mohammed aged 10 years. He is a friend of Hassan, Amina and Aysha and lives in the same street as them. Mohammed has relatives who live in the next town. Like many Somalis, Mohammed also has relatives who live in the UK.

Role card

Aysha aged 11 years. She is a friend of Hassan, Amina and Mohammed and lives in the same street as them. Aysha has relatives who live in the next town and an older cousin who lives in Nairobi, the capital city of Kenya. Like many Somalis, Aysha also has relatives who live in the UK.

Chance Card A

The baggage you are carrying is too heavy. Miss a go. You have to get rid of three items. What will you choose?

Chance Card B

Blisters on feet. Miss a go.

Chance Card C

The house where you are hiding is searched by soldiers. You have to give them money. If you took money with you, stay where you are. If not, go back to the beginning.

Chance Card D

You are told that soldiers are looking for your relatives. Move to another house to hide. Miss two goes.

Chance Card E

The lorry breaks down. Miss three goes.

Chance Card F

You are stopped by soldiers. You have to give them money. Do you have any? If not, miss two goes.

Chance Card G

You run short of water. Miss two goes.

Chance Card H

You see planes fly overhead. Hide in the bushes. Miss a go.

77

Chance Card I
You pass fruit trees. Have an extra go.

Chance Card M
Food and medicine reach the camp. Have an extra go.

Chance Card Q
You cannot find Aysha's cousin's house. Miss two goes.

Chance Card J
Stand on a land mine at the border. It explodes. You are out of the game.

Chance Card N
Your uncle in London sends a Red Cross message to you. He gives you his address and says he can help you. Go forward five places.

Chance Card R
The airline check-in staff are suspicious of your passport. They think it is forged and take it away to look at. They will not let you on the plane. Stay where you are for the rest of the game.

Chance Card K
Kenyan border guards find you. They will not let you through. Go back to 13.

Chance Card O
Wait for money in the post. Miss a go.

Chance Card S
There is no-one to meet you at the airport in London. Miss two goes.

Chance Card L
Food and medicine are in short supply in the camp. You are hungry. Your blisters have become infected. Miss two goes.

Chance Card P
The bus stop for Nairobi means a day's walk. You have to cross a river to reach it. The current is strong. You get washed down stream. Miss four goes.

Chance Card T
Meet some friends from Somalia in the street. They invite you to visit and share their meal. Have an extra go.

Chance Card U

Your uncle helps you find a place at a new school. On your first day there you make a new friend. Go forward three spaces.

Chance Card Y

Your feel homesick and miss your family very much. Miss a go.

Chance Card V

You receive a Red Cross message from your parents. They are alive and well and living in a refugee camp. You feel very happy after this news. Go forward three spaces.

Chance Card Z

You and your uncle's family have been refused permission to stay in the UK. You are put on a plane back to Kenya and then taken in a truck to the Somali border. Go back to 36.

Chance Card W

You are sent a letter from your aunt. She tells you that a school friend has been killed in Somalia. Miss two goes.

Chance Card X

You all move to a new flat. It is a much better place. Have an extra go.

Chapter Five

Refugees' Needs in a New Country

This chapter examines the needs of refugees in rich and poor countries, and how these needs are met. The chapter also aims to build empathy towards newly-arrived refugees.

Refugees arriving in the UK   HOWARD DAVIES

Activity

Refugees' needs

Time needed: 45 minutes.

The aim of the activity is to get children to examine the needs of refugees at different points in their settlement in a new country.

The children will need pens and paper. They should be divided into pairs. Each participant is to put themselves in the position of being a refugee newly arrived in Europe. The pairs should imagine they are now standing at an airport in a new country, and do not speak the language of the new country.

The pairs should make a list of things that they will need in their new country:

➤ immediately
➤ after six months

After the lists have been made the group should come together and compile class lists. The lists can be used as a prompt for discussion about the needs of refugees, or the needs of particular groups.

Discussion points

Do you think that elderly refugees have different needs to those under 50? What might they be?

Do you think that children have different needs to adult refugees? Why?

Information

Refugees in poor countries

Refugee Camps

Most refugees in poor countries live in refugee camps. Here, large numbers of people live in tents or other types of temporary shelter. Refugee camps are meant to provide for refuges who have just arrived in a new country. The camps are meant to be temporary, to meet needs for a for a short period of time. Sadly, some refugees end up living in refugee camps for many years.

Basic needs

Clean water, food and shelter are needed by everyone, not just refugees. Water is the most immediate need, as no-one can live for very long without something to drink. There are several ways of providing clean water to a refugee camp. If there are water-bearing rocks under the camp, a well can be drilled. Alteratively, water can be collected from a lake or river, purified, then taken by tanker to the camp.

Getting food to refugees in camps is another problem. Food is bulky and refugee camps are often in isolated areas, without good transport. The food that is provided should not need too much cooking or too much local firewood will be used. Often the trees around refugee camps are very quickly destroyed, causing environmental damage. Food

should also be appropriate to local tastes and must provide enough energy, protein, vitamins and minerals.

Refugees also need shelter. Even in hot climates, refugees need shelter from the sun, from the cold at night or from rain. If there is no local building material, like wood or palm leaves, the refugees will need tents and plastic sheeting brought to them.

Keeping in good health

Clinics are another important part of a refugee camp. Many new refugees are not in good health. They may have war injuries from their home countries. Often refugees have walked many miles before getting to the safety of a camp. They may not have eaten well for many weeks. One of the urgent jobs of the doctors and nurses

Burmese refugees queue for water in a camp in Bangladesh.   HOWARD DAVIES

who work in refugee camps is to treat newly-arrived refugees. Hungry children may need special meals so that they can regain the weight that they lost.

Another job that nurses do, with the help of engineers, is to make sure that there are enough wells and toilets for the refugees, and to make sure that everyone uses them. Without toilets and clean water to wash in, diseases will spread very quickly.

Schools

In camps, refugees have often been able to set up schools soon after arriving in a new country, often with very little help. Refugees who were teachers in their home country may take the lead in doing this. To help refugee teachers, organisations such as the UNICEF - the United Nations Children's Fund - have been providing 'the school in a box' to refugee teachers. The school in a box contains the basic equipment needed to set up a school, such as slates, chalk, a blackboard, exercise books and some text books. Often schools start under a tree.

Becoming self-sufficient

Refugee camps are meant to be temporary. But many refugees end up living in camps for many years. For such refugees, the chance of training and work is important. Organisations like the United Nations High Commissioner for Refugees (UNHCR) and Oxfam have started training and work projects in refugee camps. In Kenya, Somali and Sudanese refugees are now growing vegetables in gardens around their homes. Tending a garden

can ease the sense of helplessness many refugees feel. Refugees will also then be able to eat to nutritious vegetables. Looking after a kitchen garden equips young people with agricultural skills they may need when they return home.

In other parts of the world refugees have been given training in leatherwork, crafts, tailoring and mending cars.

Finding lost family

When refugees flee war and other dangers, it is easy to be parted from members of your family. Parents are often separated from

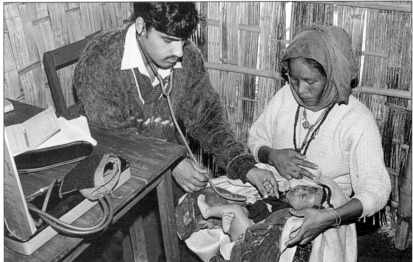
A clinic run by refugee doctors in a Bhutanese refugee camp in Nepal   UNHCR

A disabled Afghan refugee working as a tailor in a project organised by UNHCR

HOWARD DAVIES

children. The violence in Rwanda in 1994 and 1995 left over 100,000 children separated from their parents. For refugees like them, family tracing is needed. Social workers from organisations like UNHCR and the Red Cross help families find those they have lost. There are many different ways of looking for missing people. Sometimes an advertisement is placed in a newspaper or on a poster. Social workers may travel widely to look for missing people in refugee camps or squatter settlements on the outskirts of large towns. A good tracer is an imaginative person and uses the skills that a

detective would use. If family tracing is successful, divided families can be united to great joy.

Refugees in cities

Although most refugees in poor countries live in camps, a small number live in towns and cities. They may live in shanty homes at the edge of a city, often in great poverty. There are particular problems in helping refugees who live in cities, because they are scattered around. More positively, it can be easier to find work in a city.

Activity

Refugee camps

Time needed: 45 minutes.

The activity aims to help children think about the needs of refugees living in camps. It builds on some of the ideas highlighted in the activity on page xxx.

You will need to copy the information sheet Refugees in Poor Countries and prepare the cards, so that there is a set for every pair.

The information sheet about refugees in poor countries should be read to the children. Alternatively, the children can read it themselves. The class should then be divided into pairs.

The children are going to prioritise their needs having arrived in a refugee camp in a poor country.

The teacher should set the scene: the children should imagine that they are a married refugee and have four children. After fleeing a war, you have become separated from your two older children. You have now arrived in a refugee camp in a neighbouring country. Nearly 100,000 people live in the refugee camp. The local people speak a different language. Although warm in the day, the nights can be very cold in this country.

There are lots of things that a newly-arrived refugee may need in such a place. By sorting through the cards, the children are going to decide on the TEN most important things they need.

cooking pots	toilets	cash	blankets
clean water	a warm jumper	social workers to look for the missing children	a bucket
a radio	a passport	doctor and a clinic	a gun
a tent	a class for adults to learn the new language	a school	food
firewood	a cow	wood and bricks to make a permanent house.	

Information

Organisations that work with refugees

Throughout the world many different organisations are working to help refugees. Some are large but most of them are small. Some work in many different countries, others in just one country.

International organisations

The largest refugee organisation in the world is the United Nations High Commissioner for Refugees - UNHCR. It was set up by the United Nations in 1951. UNHCR's headquarters are in Geneva, Switzerland and it has offices in more than 120 countries. UNHCR has four different jobs:

➤ to make sure that refugees are not sent back to places where their lives would be in danger;
➤ to see that governments treat refugees fairly;
➤ to work with other organisations to make sure that aid reaches refugees to solve refugees' problems.

UNHCR tries to help people return home if it becomes safe for them to do so. If this is impossible, UNHCR helps people settle in a new country. Several other international organisations work with refugees. The United Nations Relief and Works Agency for Palestine Refugees in the Near East (UNRWA) works with Palestinian refugees. The United Nations Children's Fund (UNICEF) sometimes works with refugee children. The International Committee for the Red Cross often works in war zones with refugees and displaced people.

Individual governments

Individual governments may work with refugee groups in their own countries. For example, the British government paid for reception centres and help for 2,500 Bosnian refugees who arrived in 1993.

Non-governmental organisations

Non-governmental organisations, known as NGOs are not run by governments and are usually much smaller than international and government organisations. Some non-governmental organisations

Afghan refugee children in a camp in Pakistan

HOWARD DAVIES

THE REFUGEE COUNCIL

THE REFUGEE COUNCIL HELPS REFUGEES FROM MANY DIFFERENT COUNTRIES. ITS OFFICES ARE IN LONDON AND ABOUT 200 PEOPLE WORK AT THE REFUGEE COUNCIL

THE REFUGEE COUNCIL GIVES ADVICE TO REFUGEES. IT EXPLAINS TO THEM HOW THEY CAN FIND A HOUSE AND A SCHOOL FOR THEIR CHILDREN.

THE REFUGEE COUNCIL TRAINS REFUGEES SO THEY WILL FIND IT EASIER TO FIND WORK.

THE REFUGEE COUNCIL HAS JUST BUILT A HOME FOR REFUGEE CHILDREN WHO HAVE COME TO BRITAIN BY THEMSELVES. THE REFUGEE COUNCIL IS TAKING CARE OF ABOUT 20 REFUGEE CHILDREN WITHOUT PARENTS.

THE REFUGEE COUNCIL WRITES BOOKS AND LEAFLETS ABOUT REFUGEES. THESE BOOKS EXPLAIN ABOUT REFUGEES, AND HELP PEOPLE IN BRITAIN UNDERSTAND WHY PEOPLE LEAVE THEIR HOME COUNTRIES.

work with refugees in poor countries. This group of organisations are sometimes know as overseas aid agencies. Oxfam and the Save the Children Fund are two examples of overseas aid agencies. They are working with all the major refugee groups in today's world, as well as many other poor people. Overseas agencies do receive small amounts of money from governments but for most of their work they rely on money from ordinary people.

Helping refugees in the UK

There are over 300 non-governmental organisations working with refugees in Britain. They include large organisations like the Refugee Council and small self-help groups.

The Refugee Council

The Refugee Council was set up in 1951. Today 160 staff and over 100 volunteers work in its offices.

Self help

Throughout the world, in rich and poor countries, refugees are active in helping themselves. There are about 280 refugee self-help groups in the UK, sometimes called refugee community organisations.

Refugee self-help groups are usually small. Only one or two people may work for them. They are run by refugees themselves. Refugee self help groups are also places where refugees can meet other people from the home country and make new friends. For isolated refugees this is very important.

Refugees often need *information and advice*. They might need advice on finding somewhere to live or how to get their children into school.

Finding work is also important.

An English class for older Armenian refugees in London   HOWARD DAVIES

Self help groups may offer *careers advice* and English language classes, or small-scale *training for work*. Some refugees find it difficult to cope in a new country, because of past experiences or the huge changes in their lives. Many self help groups offer *counselling* for refugees who have had terrible experiences or are finding life difficult.

Some groups of refugees are more needy. *Elderly refugees or unaccompanied refugee children* may need special help. Self-help groups may run activities for older people such as lunch clubs or youth clubs for unaccompanied refugee children.

Almost all refugee self help groups organise *cultural activities* such as religious celebrations or musical performances.

Finally, refugee self help groups work with young people. They run *youth clubs* and *mother tongue schools* for children so that they can learn the language of their home country.

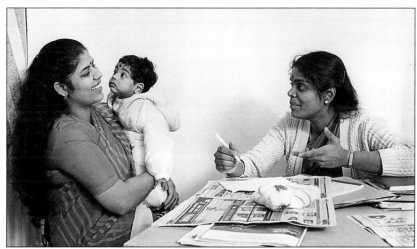

A refugee mother receives help at a Tamil self-help group   CAROLINE PENN

Activity

Researching organisations that work with refugees

Children can be encouraged to find out more about organisations that work with refugees. They can write off to some of the organisations listed at the end of this book to find out about their work. Representatives from local and national refugee organisations can be invited into school to talk to the children.

Information

Refugees in rich countries

Most of the world's refugees live in poor countries, but every year refugees also flee to the rich countries of Europe, North America and Australia. Here they face a different set of problems to those refugees living in the poorer countries of the world. In many parts of the rich world refugees have been made to feel unwelcome, by both governments and ordinary people.

Governments of rich countries have made it more difficult for refugees to enter their countries. Newly-arrived refugees have also lost their rights to permanent housing, work and college education in some countries. Governments argue that restricting the rights of newly-arrived refugees prevents people being tempted to move from their homes to come to rich countries. But cutting rights to housing, work and college education has made it more difficult for refugees to rebuild their lives.

Bullying

Refugees have also been made scapegoats by some politicians and newspapers. They have been blamed for causing social problems such as unemployment and homelessness. Throughout the rich world the general public has become more hostile to refugees, without really understanding the dangers that caused them to flee. Refugee children even face hostility in schools. They often tell of bullying they faced, just because they were refugees and were seen as different.

Dictionary

A **scapegoat** is a person or a group of people who are easily blamed for a problem they have not directly caused. You may have a scapegoat in your school. Refugees are scapegoats when they are blamed for causing housing shortages.

Information

Refugees in Europe

Austria

Total Population 8.1 million
Number of new refugees in 1997 6,719
Main groups Refugees from Iraq, Bosnia and Kosova

Belgium

Total Population 10.2 million
Number of new refugees, 1997 11,575
Main groups Refugees from Bosnia, Kosova and Congo (Zaire)

Denmark

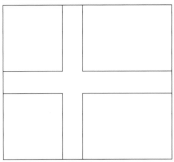

Total Population 5.3 million

Number of new refugees, 1997 5,100
Main groups Somalis, Sri Lankan Tamils, Iraqis, Palestinians and Bosnians

Finland

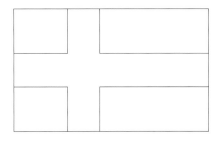

Total Population 5.1 million
Number of new refugees, 1997 973
Main groups Somalis, Vietnamese, Kurds and Bosnians

France

Total Population 58.6 million
Number of new refugees, 1997 19,983
Main groups Sri Lankan Tamils, Kurds, Vietnamese, Congolese (Zaireans), Bosnians, Algerians

Germany

Total Population 82.0 million
Number of new refugees, 1997 104,353
Main groups Germany has the largest refugee population in Europe. Refugees from many different countries live in Germany. The largest refugee groups are Turkish Kurds, Bosnians, Kosova Albanians, Iraqis, Afghans and Sri Lankans.

Greece

Total Population 10.5 million

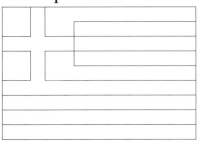

Number of new refugees, 1997 4,157
Main groups Kurds, Iranians, and Kosova Albanians.

Ireland

Total Population 3.6 million

Number of new refugees, 1997 3,883
Main groups Cubans, Bosnians, eastern European Roma.

Italy

Total Population 57.4 million

Number of new refugees, 1997 1,436
Main groups Albanians, Bosnians, Kosova Albanians and other refugees from the former Yugoslavia, Somalis, Ethiopians and Iraqis.

Luxembourg

Total Population 400,000
Number of new refugees, 1997 443
Main groups Albanians, Bosnians and Kosova Albanians

Netherlands

Total Population 15.6 million
Number of new refugees, 1997 34,443
Main groups Iraqis, Afghans, Iranians, Sri Lankans, Kurds, Somalis, Bosnians, Kosova Albanians and other refugees from the former Yugoslavia.

Portugal

Total Population 9.9 million
Number of new refugees, 1997 393
Main group Angolans

Spain

Total Population 39.3 million
Number of new refugees, 1997 4,975
Main groups Algerians, Cubans, Colombians, Iranians, Iraqis, Nigerians, Sierra Leoneans, eastern European Roma

Sweden

Total Population 8.9 million
Number of new refugees, 1997 9,619
Main groups Bosnians, Kosova Albanians, Iraqis, Somalis and Turkish Kurds.

UK

Total Population 59 million
Number of new refugees, 1997 32,500
Main groups Somalis, Sri Lankan Tamils, Kurds and Kosovans

Activity

A map of Europe

Time needed: one hour or longer.

You will need to photocopy a map of Europe and information about refugees in Europe. The children will need crayons, scissors and glue. The children should also have access to an atlas and a book or poster of different flags.

The children are going to make a display about refugees in European Union countries. They should shade in the flags. Using the information above, the children should transfer it on to a map of Europe. Other information and photographs can be added to the display.

Testimony

Quang Bui, a refugee in Sweden

Quang Bui's brother escaped from Vietnam by boat and was allowed to settle in Sweden as a refugee. Quang Bui and his parents were later allowed to join him.

"My parents are not as strict as other Vietnamese parents. I don't know what they think. I think they like living here.

I've been here a long time - eight years in fact. I know almost everyone, and indeed enjoy living here. Sometimes I ask friends to come fishing with me. We make a barbecue, we play cards and we fish.

When I first came there were some Swedish blokes, a bit older. They called us 'yellow necks', but we, the Vietnamese, helped each other. We stood up against them. We stuck together, because there were not so many of us in Sweden. Nowadays in the high school there is no problem. We all mix together. They are a great crowd and I'm good friends with everyone.

At the leisure centre you can see your friends, play cards, pool or table tennis. There should be more places for the young people - for instance leisure centres open till late at night, and Macdonalds which everyone likes and a night cafe and a disco.

Where I am living there is a place where you can play pool. You can sing Karoake in Vietnamese. You can talk with friends and eat Vietnamese food. But when I am there I don't usually sing. I don't dare!"

Information

Vietnam and Vietnamese refugees

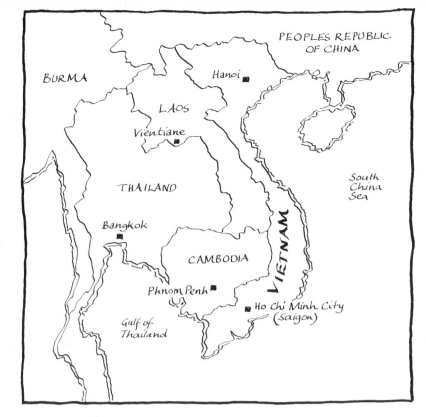

Capital Hanoi
Population 75.1 m

Vietnam was a French colony from 1887 until 1954. In 1946 a group of Vietnamese led by Ho Chi Minh started fighting for an independent, communist Vietnam. Between 1946 and 1954, over 172,000 French soldiers were killed in Vietnam.

In 1954, Vietnam was divided into two countries. The communists were to rule to rule the North. South Vietnam became a separate country. The USA, fearing a communist takeover in South Asia, provided weapons to the South Vietnamese. By 1961 US soldiers were fighting in Vietnam. The war soon got worse. Between 1968 and 1973 nearly two million Vietnamese were killed. Cambodia and Laos were also heavily bombed by the US Air Force.

In 1973 US soldiers left Vietnam. But the North and South Vietnamese armies continued fighting until 1975. In that year, the North Vietnamese army reach Saigon and the South Vietnamese government collapsed.

The first refugees to leave Vietnam were 130,000 South Vietnamese who worked for their government or had close contacts with the US. In 1977, another group of refugees left, many by boat. Many of them were opponents of the new government. In 1978 ethnic Chinese started leaving Vietnam, after anti-Chinese racism increased. They fled to China and other South East Asian countries.

The refugees left by land and sea. The boat journey was particularly dangerous and many Vietnamese refuges died at sea, by drowning or thirst.

Between 1979 and 1992 small numbers of Vietnamese refugees were invited to come and live in European countries, Australia, New Zealand, Canada and the USA. About 24,000 Vietnamese refugees settled in the UK. Many of these refugees have now had children.

A Vietnamese restaurant. Howard Davies.

Cards for Tet   HOWARD DAVIES

Information

Tet celebrations

Tet is the New Year festival of the Vietnamese people. It usually falls at the end of January or the beginning of February. This is springtime in Vietnam. Tet is celebrated by all religious groups in Vietnam. It is meant to help people begin the New Year with good intentions.

The last day of the year

Tet celebrations last three days, although the preparations start months in advance. Food for Tet is cooked in advance. The food includes rice cakes, preserved fruit and Vietnamese spring rolls.

People try and make sure that their debts are paid off by the last day of the year. They take their last bath of the year and put on new clothes. Some families set up a little altar in their homes. At midnight on the last day of the year, the father asks the God of the Old Year to hand over power to the God of the New Year. Fireworks mark the beginning of the New Year.

The first day of Tet

Everyone wears their best clothes. Grandparents and other elderly members of the family come to the homes of their children and grandchildren. The family then does something called *mung tuoi* or *li xi* in southern Vietnam. The grandparents sit in the family sitting room. The children and grandchildren then tell them of their wishes for the New Year. After this, the grandparents give out small red envelopes containing money. It is like a birthday for everyone.

The first person who visits the home in the New Year is very important. If the first visitor is happy, the New Year will be happy. If the visitor is sad, then the next year will be sad. When the first visitor arrives, he or she is given special Tet food.

The second and third days of Tet

Everyone visits friends and relatives on these days. There are also public celebrations. In Vietnam travelling theatres visit villages and there is a lot of singing and dancing.

Many people play a game at Tet. The game is Vietnamese Animal Chess and is called *Bau Ca Tom Cua* in Vietnamese. You can buy the game in Vietnamese shops in the UK, but it is also fun to make your own set.

The legend of the firecracker

A special Tet story

Tet is celebrated with firecrackers that make loud bangs. This is why.....

In ancient times there were two wicked spirits who hated people and played nasty tricks on them. Both of them did not like light or noise, so they did their dirty deeds at night.

At Tet all good spirits have to report to heaven. But one New Year the wicked spirits were in a particularly bad mood. Their tricks were making people frightened and angry.

But one clever person learned that the wicked spirits were frightened of light and noise. So everyone decided to light up their homes and let off firecrackers. This scared away the wicked spirits.

The people kept lighting firecrackers until Tet was over and the good spirits had returned from heaven. To this day at Tet people light up their houses and let off firecrackers.

Activity

Finding out about other New Year festivals

Time needed: lesson and library time and homework time for research.

This is a research activity, where children are encouraged to look at the different ways that people celebrate New Year.

All communities have New Year celebrations. Different people celebrate New Year in different ways. Some people may also celebrate two New Years. For example, Jewish families may celebrate Rosh HaShanah - Jewish New Year, and the beginning of the European calendar year on 1st January.

The children should be given two tasks. They should be asked to find out and write about how their own family celebrates New Year. Then using library books or by interviewing friends they should find out about other New Year festivals.

Using the information they have found they should complete two pieces of writing.

1. At New Year my family ....
2. I found out about other New Year festivals.

Different New Year Festivals ❧ Hogmanay - Scotland ❧ Chinese New Year ❧ Tet - Vietnamese New Year ❧ Nawroz - Kurdish and Persian New Year ❧ Rosh HaShanah - Jewish New Year ❧ The Day of Hijrah - Islamic New Year ❧ Maskaram I - Ethiopian New Year ❧ Diwali Festival and New Year - the Hindu New Year

---

Activity

Make your own Vietnamese animal chess game

Time needed: one hour.

Many people play Vietnamese Animal Chess during the Tet celebrations. You can buy the game in Vietnamese shops, but it is also fun for children to make their own sets.

You will need felt pens, glue, cardboard (at least A4 in size), scissors, large dice and small sticky labels. Divide the class into groups of four.

Making the game

1. The children should first make their board. Divide the A4 card into six squares. In successive squares they should draw a deer, bottle, hen, fish, crab and lobster.

2. Make 100 tokens out of the card. The children can make them look like money.

3. On each small sticky label write the letters 'D', 'B', 'H', 'F', 'C' and 'L'. These stand for deer, bottle, hen, fish, crab and lobster. Stick each label over one side of the dice. You can buy special dice from Vietnamese shops which have these items printed on instead of numbers. If you live near such a shop this will save you changing your dice.

Playing the game

4. In the groups, one person should take the role of the banker. That person should be given all the tokens. The banker then gives each of the three players ten tokens each.

DEER   BOTTLE   HEN

FISH   CRAB   LOBSTER

5. The players then put one or more tokens on the picture of their choice. Each player then shakes the dice. If the picture on the dice matches where the player put his or her token, the banker pays that player a sum equal to the number of tokens put down on that square. For example, if you put two tokens down on the hen, and then you shook the hen, the banker would pay you two extra tokens.

6. If the pictures do not match, the banker receives the tokens that are on the square.

7. The game ends when all the players apart from one have run out of tokens. The winner is the person who has some tokens left.

Information

Refugees in the UK

Country of origin	Main dates of entry	Numbers of refugees
Protestant refugees from the Spanish Netherlands and France	1560-1700	150,000
Jews from Poland, Russia, Austria and Romania	1880-1914	200,000
Belgians	1914-1918	250,000
Germany, Austria and Czechoslovakia	1933-1939	56,000
Basque refugee children	1937	4,000
Poland	1939-1950	250,000
Other European refugees from the Nazis	1940-1945	100,000
Czechoslovakia, Hungary and Romania	1945-1950	50,000
Hungary	1956	17,000
Czechoslovakia	1968	5,000
Uganda	1972-	37,000
Chile	1973-79	3,000
Ethiopia and Eritrea	1973-	17,000
Cyprus	1974	24,000
Vietnam	1975-1992	24,000
Iran	1978-	24,000
Afghanistan	1979-	8,000
Iraq	1980-	18,000
Ghana	1982-1996	17,000
Sri Lanka (Tamils)	1983-	33,000
Pakistan	1984-	6,000
Somalia	1988-	70,000
Turkey (Kurds)	1989-	30,000
Congo (Zaire)	1989-	19,000
Sudan	1989-	6,000
Angola	1990-	12,000
Bosnia	1992-1996	9,000
Sierra Leone	1993-	7,000
Kenya	1994-	6,000
Algeria	1994-	7,000
Nigeria	1994-	8,000
Yugoslavia (Kosova Albanians)	1995-	12,000
Colombia	1996-	7,000

Activity

Refugees in the UK

Fill in the missing words to learn more about refugees
in the UK.

In 1997 some ——— new refugees arrived in the UK.
They came from many different countries, but the main
groups of refugees who have arrived recently are
Somalis, Kosova Albanians, ——— refugees from Iraq
and ——— and Sri Lankan Tamils. Four refugees out of
five live in London.

Life is not always easy for newly-arrived refugees in the
UK. Since 1996 many new refugees have been unable to
get social security. Instead they have been given ———
or supermarket vouchers so that they do go hungry.
This group of refugees do not have extra money to buy
things like ——— and shoes. Life is very hard for them.

Refugees also have to find a place to live, to learn ——
— (if they do not speak it already) and to find a ———.
Children need to find a new ——— and to learn
English. Refugee children also need to make new
friends and to feel at home in their new school.

Refugees are not always welcome in their new homes.
Some newspapers have said that refugees come to the
UK for a better life, without giving information about
the reasons they fled from their own countries.
Newspaper articles have also blamed refugees for ———
——— shortages. These articles have affected what
ordinary people think of refugees.

❧ 32,500 ❧ Kurdish ❧ Turkey ❧ school ❧ food parcels
❧ English ❧ housing ❧ clothes ❧ job

Testimony

Nathaniel's diary

Nathaniel is 33 years old. He is a refugee from the Democratic Republic of Congo (an African country formerly known as Zaire). Before he came to the UK he was arrested and very badly treated in his home country.

Nathaniel's first languages are Lingala and French. Because he cannot speak much English he cannot get a job. Some groups of refugees in the UK are not allowed to collect social security. Nathaniel is one of them. His rent and electricity bills are paid for him and he gets vouchers for food that he can use at his supermarket. The vouchers are for £28 a week and are meant to cover all Nathaniel's needs.

11am

I have a shower and a cup of tea. I don't sleep well at night, and as usual I have not slept. When I first came to England, I got benefits and I could learn English. I also did a computing course. I could go out sometimes because I had the money to travel. But now my benefits have stopped. I can't go to college to learn English, or take public transport.

12 noon

I walk to the Medical Foundation. I have been coming here to see doctors about my injuries from my arrest in Zaire. I am having treatment on my right arm, I could not lift it when I arrived. I also have trouble with my eyes.

6 pm

Back at the flat, I talk to my flatmate who arrived here with me from the Congo. We knew each other as students. We are doing nothing now. It is difficult to get a job.

8 pm

Have a bath. I get lonely and used to watch a lot of TV, but now I don't get benefits, I can't afford to pay for a TV licence. Last week my electricity was cut off because the council forgot to pay my bill.

9 pm

I read a book in bed. I keep an English-to-French dictionary beside me. I enjoy learning English. I studied politics and economics in the Congo. I wanted to work in government to try and improve my country. Congo could be a rich country if the government was good.

1 am

I keep reading until I finish the book. I have to leave the light on at night or I get nightmares. I think about my family all the time and miss them. I have no way of contacting them, but I have heard that my mother is alive and in Zambia.

Information

Democratic Republic of Congo

(formerly Zaire)

Capital Kinshasa
Population 48 million
Languages French, Lingala, Kikongo, Tshiluba, Swahili and 200 other languages and dialects.
Main exports Copper, palm oil and coffee.

The Democratic Republic of Congo is one of the largest countries in Africa. Much of the country is rain forest. The Republic of Congo also contains rich mineral reserves. The country is the world's largest producer of copper. However, most people who live in the Republic of Congo are very poor. This is because money from the sale of copper has been taken by a very small number of people.

The Republic of Congo became independent in 1960. President Mobutu ruled the country from 1965 until 1997. He renamed the country Zaire in 1971. Mobutu did not rule well, and took a lot of the money from the sale of copper for himself. President Mobutu's government did not spend money on developing the country. Very little money was spent building school, hospitals and roads at this time.

People who did not agreed with President Mobutu faced many dangers. They were imprisoned, or beaten by soldiers and security officers. People fled as refugees, because their lives were in danger. Over 10,000 refugees from the Democratic Republic of Congo fled to the UK.

In 1997 guerrillas who supported Laurence Kabila started fighting in the east of the country. The Congolese people decided that they had had enough. They gave their support to Laurence Kabila. He became the new President after President Mobutu escaped from the country. Peace did not last long. Soldiers opposed to Laurence Kabila began fighting again in 1998.

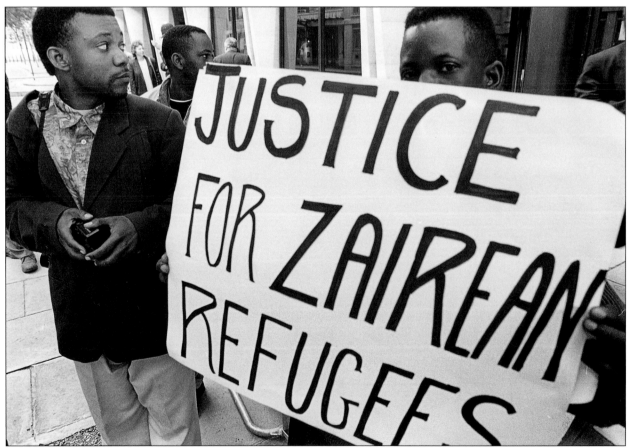

Refugees from Congo (Zaire) in London

JON WALTER

Activity

Comparing Nathaniel's day with mine

Time needed: 45 minutes.

All the children will need copies of Nathaniel's story and the 24 hour time clocks. Nathaniel's day has been shaded on to one of the time clocks. The children should use the same shading and represent their own day on the clock.

The time clocks should be used as a prompt to talk about how Nathaniel's day is different from theirs.

❧ Sleeping ❧ Washing and dressing. ❧ School or college ❧ Reading ❧ Eating ❧ Playing ❧ Working ❧ Visits

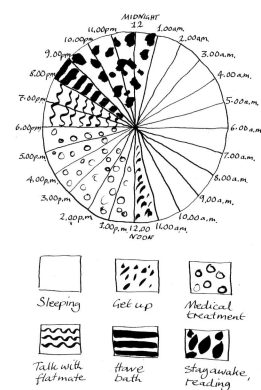

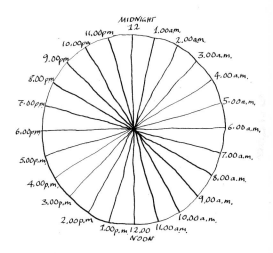

Activity

Presenting information

Time needed: two hours.

The activity aims to develop children's presentational skills.

The class should be divided into threes or fours. Using the country information provided in Chapters Three, Four and Five, library books, newspaper articles and any other resources, including parents, the groups should each be allocated a refugee producing country. The children should work in their groups to prepare a three minute verbal presentation about each country. The presentations should include information about the country's geography, history, culture and present events. The presentations should include positive material, as well as information about the conflicts in these countries. Parents and community representatives can be invited in and interviewed as part of the research process.

Information

Refugee children's education

For refugees, both adults and children, education is often the route to rebuilding their lives in a new country. But many refugee children do not go to school. Only 12 per cent of the world's refugee children are presently receiving an education. Organisations like the United Nations High Commissioner for Refugees (UNHCR) are now working to ensure that more refugee children will be able to go to school.

It is important that refugee children can go to school as soon as possible after leaving their home country - even if this means a school under a tree in a refugee camp. For children who have fled fighting, a school can give a child a chance of a more normal life, and the chance to make new friends.

The benefits of schooling

Among teenagers, particularly boys, the chance to go to school can take the pressure away from being a child soldier. In countries such as Afghanistan, Angola, Liberia, Mali, Sierra Leone, Somali, Sri Lanka and Sudan, children as young as ten may be encouraged to fight. Education can offer an alternative future to that of being a child soldier. Schools can also deliver

A Burmese refugee boy in a school in a refugee camp   HOWARD DAVIES

messages important to the survival of newly-arrived refugees. In refugee camps, schools have been used to deliver messages about health care, family tracing and land mine awareness. For example, schools in Rwandan refugee camps in Tanzania were used to deliver messages about the prevention of diseases.

Schools can free mothers of child care, enabling them to work. This may be important in refugee camps where there are large number of single mothers - refugee communities where men have been killed in fighting.

In the long term schools can be used to try and solve the conflicts that cause people to become refugees. Dance, drama, music, sport and discussion can be used to bring young people of different ethnic groups together, and to break down hatreds that cause wars. In parts of the world like Bosnia and Burundi there are many small

organisations working with children to break down the hatreds that cause war.

Practical issues

In camps in Africa and Asia refugees have often been able to set up schools soon after arriving in a new country, often with very little help. Refugees who were teachers in their home country often take the lead in doing this. To help refugee teachers do this, aid organisations such as the UNICEF - the United Nations Children's Fund - have been providing 'the school in a box' to volunteer refugee teachers. The school in a box contains the basic equipment needed to set up a school, such as slates, chalk, a blackboard, exercise books and some text books.

In rich countries, refugee children usually attend the same schools as any other child. Here refugee children face a different set of challenges. They have to learn a new language very quickly.

Sometimes, the memories of what happened at home can make it difficult to concentrate on lessons. Sadly, refugee children sometimes face bullying in new schools. But given sympathy and help, refugee children are often very successful in their new schools.

Mother tongue schools

At weekends and evenings in countries like the UK, refugee children can be found learning their first language, in living rooms, halls and empty school buildings. They are students in mother tongue schools, run by refugees themselves.

Refugee children at a London school with their friends   HOWARD DAVIES

Going to school on Saturday may seem like a bad idea, but there are many benefits for refugee children. It is always useful to know two languages rather than one. Mother tongue schools enable refugee children to meet others from a similar background, and to talk about things that are important in their lives. For refugee children knowing how to read and write your first language is important, if one day, you might wish to return to your home country.

The teachers in mother tongue schools are usually volunteers. Parents may help run the school, helping in class and in sports and cultural events.

There are mother tongue schools in most countries which have a large refugee populations. There are over 100 mother tongue schools run by refugees living in the UK. In Denmark, Finland, Norway and Sweden, refugee children are allowed to learn their first language during school time, rather than at weekends. The governments in these countries pay for refugee children to learn their home language.

An Afghan mother tongue school in London. This school also teaches Afghan dancing
HOWARD DAVIES

109

Metin, Serpil and Choman start school

Metin is a Kurdish boy from Turkey. He is now 12 years old.

"When we came to England we stayed with out friends, all our family stayed in one room. We didn't go out that much and the room was very small. We were there for about a month, I think. I knew my mum didn't have any money for the things I wanted, so I didn't ask for anything. But I wanted some toys and games and other things.

I wanted to go to school, but my first day at school, I cried as I didn't want to be there. I didn't make any friends, nothing. I didn't understand anything and I didn't have any friends. I thought I would understand the teacher, but I didn't. My face was red, I think. After some time because I didn't understand any English, they took me to a special class."

Serpil is a Kurdish girl from Turkey. She is now 11. Here she explains what it was like to start her new school.

"Everybody kept staring at me. I was embarrassed and shy. Even at dinnertime I was scared to have my dinner. They were talking about me. I know they were talking about me because they were calling my name. I was really upset then.

I told my Mum and Dad and they told me when I get to learn English they wouldn't say anything to you. I kept crying and said to my Dad, "I don't want to go to school, I don't want to see them laughing at me and see them talking about me."

I had two Turkish friends at school, but not that close. Sometimes they helped me, but most of the time they didn't. When they translated anything they were

embarrassed. They were embarrassed that the other kids would say, "Don't talk to that girl, she doesn't speak English.

Teachers were always helping me with my work. There was a separate teacher who came to help me. I really liked that teacher. I was happiest with her and not with the children in the class."

Choman is 18 years old. She is also Kurdish and was born in Iraqi Kurdistan. Here she describes how it feels to arrive in Britain as a refugee.

"Two years ago, on a misty evening in September I arrived at Heathrow airport, alone and scared, but full of hope. I was happy as I was going to be with my parents again after being away from them for over a year.

I was so happy about starting school and learning English. I had been away from school for two years because we were travelling and did not have a permanent place to live. I promised myself not to miss school again and not to waste more time. I had to be serious and work hard, there was no time for being lazy. So, ten days after my arrival I started going to a school close to my house, called Hampstead School.

The problem was that at my age I should have been doing A-Levels, but because I didn't speak any English they put me in Year Ten with students who were three years younger than me. The teachers didn't believe that I would be able to do GCSEs with so little English. I was told that the best thing for me was to stay in Year Ten until my English was better and maybe in two years I could attempt GCSEs.

Being with younger people is not a problem if they are

mature. But when you are a teenager a three year difference is quite a big gap, especially if you don't speak the language and you are new to the culture. It is at this time that you need friends the most. But I was shocked to find out that in the lunch queue they used to laugh at me and say that I never had decent food in my country. They said I had always been hungry that's why I ran away from my home. Some people treated me like a fool because I couldn't speak English well, some just ignored me as if I didn't exist.

Nobody wanted to sit next to me in lessons and no-one wanted to have me as their partner in PE. I was all alone in the corner and did not understand the jokes during the lessons. I couldn't understand the subjects we studied because of my English and could never express myself during any simple discussion. I was too scared to talk because I knew that if I made a mistake some of them would laugh at me. Once I even got beaten up by a group of students who used to bully everyone. They beat me one evening when I was walking home alone. They said they couldn't stand me because I was a refugee who lived on the Government's money (which they considered to be their own money). After this I lost all my confidence and began to think that I was the most unwanted person on earth. I used to cry on my own and thought about leaving school. I started to believe that what other people thought about me was true.

I almost gave up. The reason that I didn't was because of my mother's help and the support I got from my teachers. So there was still hope. There were people who cared and helped, so I carried on. I had to anyway because I believe life is a fight. I managed to do three GCSEs eight months after my arrival which I counted as a big success. Now I am doing three A-Levels in maths, physics and art. I speak English quite well and sometimes I write poetry in English, other times I translate my poems from my language. I have some published work and I have made a few nice friends who can accept me as I am."

Activity

How does it feel to be new?

Time needed: one hour.

The activity aims to develop empathy towards newly-arrived refugee children.

Each child will need paper and pens.

The class should be asked to imagine what it would be like to arrive in UK from another country. Each child can decide from which country they have come. In small groups the children can discuss their arrival in Britain, the new home, the first day at school and other new experiences. Children's own experiences of starting school can be used as a prompt for discussion. There may be children in the class who did not speak English when they started school and their experiences should be utilised.

Each child should then write a letter to an imaginary friend they left in their home country. The letter should describe how it feels to be living in a new country and starting a new school.

This activity can be adapted for use with very young children. They can discuss what it might feel like to arrive in a new country and a new school. Their responses can be recorded on a cassette recorder.

Activity

Learning from refugee children

The aim of the activity is to help children understand and empathise with refugees in Britain. You may need to photocopy the testimonies of refugee children in the UK. The testimonies should be read to the class, or read by the children or groups of children. The testimonies should be used as a basis for a class discussion about the experiences of refugees in the UK, or a piece of writing.

Children can consider the following points.

➤ What happened to Metin, Serpil and Choman when they started school?

➤ How did Metin, Serpil and Choman find their new schools?

➤ What might schools and school pupils do to make things easier and happier for refugee children?

Activity

Learning a new language

This activity aims to help children empathise with newly-arrived refugee children who don't speak English.

If you don't speak another language, you will need the help of another teacher, parent or helper who speaks another language that won't be understood by most children in the class. The helper or teacher should be invited into the class. Their task is to teach about 10 minutes of a lesson, using another language. After this is finished, the children should be asked what it felt like to be taught in a language they did not understand. This can be followed up with writing.

Information

Unaccompanied refugee children

The most needy of all refugees are unaccompanied refugee children. These are refugee children who have become separated from their parents and have no other close relative who can care for them. Some unaccompanied refugee children get split up from their parents in the chaos of running away from fighting. Other refugee children are deliberately sent away by their parents, when it becomes too dangerous at home.

Today nearly 650,000 of the world's refugees are unaccompanied children. The largest group of unaccompanied children are from Rwanda. Over 100,000 Rwandan children became separated from their families in 1994 and 1995. In Europe, the largest group of unaccompanied refugee children are Albanian boys from Kosova in the Federal Republic of Yugoslavia. Their parents have sent them to safety in countries such as the UK and Germany, so that the boys are not forced to serve in the army.

The right kind of help
Unaccompanied refugee children need food, clothing,

Unaccompanied Rwandan children in Congo   UNHCR

shelter and care, like any other children. Most of the world's unaccompanied children are cared for in children's homes. But there are other ways of providing care. Organisations that work with refugees sometimes try and find foster parents for unaccompanied children.

Another way of helping older unaccompanied refugee children is to set up group homes. Here four or five children live together. They cook and do their own housework. Once or twice a week a social worker visits the group home to see if everyone is well.

Many unaccompanied refugee children need help in finding lost parents. Social workers from organisations like the Red Cross help unaccompanied children find their families. This task is called family tracing. The

family tracer uses the skills that a detective would use, to look for lost family members. If an unaccompanied child's parents are found, that child can usually return home.

Painful memories
Sadly, many unaccomapnied children have hidden scars. They may have had terrifying experience such as seeing a member of their family being killed. Other children may not know if their parents are alive or dead and be very worried about them. All refugee children will miss relatives, friends, their toys and other familiar things. Refugee children may need special help to overcome painful memories. Being able to talk about your problems to a social worker may be helpful. Other refugee children find that painting or writing helps them come to terms with painful memories.

Arthur's story

Artur is a 17 year old refugee who has managed to tun his life into a success story. He was born in Angola where there has been fighting since 1961.

Artur remembers the fighting coming to his home town. Chaos broke out at school. When he returned home his house had been bombed and there was no trace of his parents our younger sister. He and his brother were helped to escape to the UK. On arrival he was lucky. He was taken to Korczak House, a children's home for unaccompanied refugees. He is now living in another home called the Cedars. This home is run by the Refugee Council and prepares unaccompanied refugee children and young people for independent life. Young refugees learn how to cook, manage their money and other skills a person need to live alone.

Artur is studying at a local college. He also plays football for Wimbledon Under 18s and looks set for a career as a professional footballer. This is what Artur has to say:

"We were frightened when we got to England. But we were taken to Korczak House and I loved it there. I felt protected. I couldn't speak any English when I first came. I used to get bullied at school. But I worked very hard and passed my examinations. I am now studying French and Spanish at college. The Cedars is a good place to live because of the staff and the atmosphere. I like my bedroom, it's like having my own house. I feel more in control of my life there. We do our own cooking and cleaning.

I've always loved sport. I played a short time for West Ham and since July I've been playing for Wimbledon. Playing football has been my dream since I've been very young.

Life is still difficult at times, especially when I think of my family. But I just think to myself that I have to be strong. I don't want to waste my time here. I love my family and if they are still alive I want to concentrate my life to help them. I'd like to go back to Angola one day. But England would definitely be my second home."

Activity

What does home mean to me?

Time needed: one hour.

Each child will need a large piece of drawing paper and coloured pencils or felt pens. In the middle of the paper, the children should draw a picture of their home town or village. Around the outside they should draw pictures of the things and people that they value most about their home area. For example, children could draw certain people, places, objects, feelings or memories.

The children should then come together as a whole class. Some of the pictures can be pinned up to prompt a discussion about what home means to different people. The class can also discuss the feelings they would have about home if they had to move to another country. Artur's story can be introduced to stimulate discussion about peope who feel they have two homes.

Artur's story can be also be used to prompt discussion and creative work on the needs of refugee children who arrive by themselves.

Chapter Six

Thinking About How We Receive Refugees

This chapter aims to help young children start to understand how ethnic minority groups, including refugees are received in the UK.

Through the use of activities, the chapter aims:

❧ to help children understand and celebrate cultural diversity;

❧ to be aware of their own identity; and

❧ to challenge some of the prejudices that they may have towards refugees and other minority groups.

Kurdish refugees in their new home   KAREN ROBINSON

Activity

What go we think about refugees?

Time needed: 45 minutes and homework time.

The activity is an opinion poll, designed to help children research how much people know about refugees and what they feel about them. The opinion poll survey can be kept and used as a point of reference after the class carry out more work about refugees.

Each child should have five copies of the opinion poll, pens and a clipboard. The children will also need paper and other materials if they are to present the results of their poll.

The teacher should explain the activity. Children are to carry out an opinion poll among their friends to find out their feelings towards refugees. Children should select friends from other classes or schools.

Every child should have five copies of the poll. Homework time should be allocated to complete the exercise. After the opinion polls are filled in, the class should present and analyse the results. Children can present their results as pictograms. The opinion poll results can be used to prompt discussion.

The activity 'Who Influences My Ideas' on page 132 can be used to follow up the opinion poll.

Discussion points

❥ Did any of the results of the opinion poll surprise you?

❥ How many people though that too many refugees came to the UK?

1. Give your own definition of who you think refugees are

_____

_____

_____

_____

2. Most refugees live in rich countries true/false?

3. How many refugees are there in today's world. Is it

❏ about 1,000,000 people
❏ about 6,000,000 people
❏ about 14,000,000 people
❏ about 280,000,000 people

4. How many refugees arrived in the UK in 1997?
Was it

❏ 8,000
❏ 16,000
❏ 32,000
❏ 96,000
❏ 320,000

5. Would you say that the numbers of refugees coming to the UK every year is

❏ too high
❏ about right
❏ too low
❏ don't know

Answers to questions 2,3 and 4

2. About 80% of the world's refugees live in poor countries.

3. There are about 14 million refugees in today's world.

4. Some 32,500 new refugees came to the UK in 1997.

The next eight activities aim to help young children celebrate cultural diversity.

Activity

Ways we are same and ways we are diffferent

Time needed: one hour. The activity aims to highlight diversity as a positive.

The children will need paper and pens. They should be divided into groups of four. In their groups the children should make a list of ways in which people are the same. For example, they can list physical characteristics, activities, needs and future hopes. Then the children should make a list of ways in which people are different. They should include their physical characteristics, as well as hobbies, needs, future hopes, religion and so on.

This activity can be followed up with a classroom discussion about diversity and similarity.

Activity

Portraits

Time needed: 45 minutes.

You will need drawing paper and crayons. (Schools can buy special crayons that are designed to reflect all childrens' skin colour). The class should be divided into pairs. Each child should have drawing paper and crayons. The children should start off by drawing portraits of each other. When they have finished, some of the portraits should be pinned up. These can be used as a prompt to start a discussion about the ways people may be physically different and the ways they may be similar.

Activity

Different clothes for different occassions

This activity aims to make children aware of diversity in the type of clothes that people wear. You will need to collect magazines and photographs that show adults and children wearing different types of clothes, such as work clothes, clothing from different religious and ethnic groups, clothes for leisure activities and so on.

Activity

Festival calendar

Time needed: two hours.

The class needs large sheets of sugar paper, white paper, pens, paints and other art material. The children will also need access to library reading books about different religious festivals. Religious education teacher advisers can be contacted to get up-to-date information on the dates of festivals, as many of these change.

The children are going to work in pairs to make their own festival calendar. This can be laid out like a year planner or as a circular calendar. Childrens' birthdays should be included and the calendar should be decorated.

Activity

Food from around the world

This activity illustrates the growing diversity in a child's diet. A trip should be arranged to a local supermarket. The children should be divided into groups to look at different types of food such as breads, fruit and vegetables, dried food such as pasta and rice, tinned food, spices and so on. Using a work sheet, the children should write down where each food item is grown manufactured, and in which country the food is eaten.

There are many ways that this activity can be followed up. The children can carry out the following activity and make a display of the different types of food that are now eaten in family homes. The children might also want to do some cooking. Children studying history could compare their diet with that of a medieval English peasant and see how much their diet has been enriched by trade and immigration. Alternatively the children could compile a list of what they have eaten in the last three days. This can be used as a basis for seeing what proportion of their diet has been influenced by the movement of people around the world.

Activity

Collecting our favourite recipes

Time needed: homework time and presentation time in class.

The children should be given the homework task of collecting some of their favourite recipes from home. In a later lesson the children should write about their favourite foods and perhaps include recipes. The class work can be mounted and use to prompt a discussion about how different migrations of people have influenced our national diet in the UK.

Tamil refugee buying the ingredients for some home cooking   HOWARD DAVIES

125

Information

Favourite food from different countries

Fish and chips were brought to the UK in the 17th century by Jewish refugees from the Spanish Netherlands.

Potatoes, tomatoes and chillis were brought to Europe in the 15th century by explorers who sailed to South America.

Oxtail soup, many biscuit recipes and blancmange were brought to the UK by Huguenot refugees.

Bagels and potato latkes are among the Jewish foods now eaten by many people. These foods were brought to the UK at the end of the 19th century.

When did you last eat pizza? Do you know what country pizza is from? Do you know what country spaghetti comes from? Did you know that pasta was

originally a Chinese recipe, brought to Europe by Marco Polo, an explorer.

Indian food is very much part of the UK diet. But did you know that most Indian restaurants are run by people whose families originally came from Bangladesh.

Chinese food is widely eaten in the UK, with Chinese speaking

people from many different countries running restaurants. Chinese people from Hong Kong, Vietnam, Malaysia and Singapore are all involved in catering.

Food from Cyprus and Turkey

can also be bought in supermarkets and restaurants. people from Cyprus and Turkey have introduced food such as hummus, taramasalata, kebabs, pitta bread and halva to our national diet.

Activity

Finding out about my name

This is a homework activity, to be followed up with work in class. The class will need access to books about first names and family names.

The children should be asked to find out about their names. After they have done the research the children can produce a piece of writing called 'all about my name'. Children should be asked to find the answers to some of the following questions.

➤ why did my parents choose my personal name(s)?
➤ what do my personal name(s) mean?
➤ do I have any nicknames? Do I like them?
➤ what is the meaning of my family name?
➤ is my family name shared by all members of my family?
➤ has anyone in my family ever changed their personal or family name? Why?

Information

Names from around the world

Our names are very important to us. They tell us a lot about ourselves and our background.

Most people in the world have a personal name. This might have a particular meaning. A personal name might reflect the fashion at the time a child was born. A child might be named after a relative or after a famous person. Our personal name might also tell us something about when and where we were born. Our personal names might have a religious meaning. Finally, personal names might reflect cultural background.

Most, but not all people in the world, also have a family name. But different cultures have different ways of organising family names. Below is some information about some of the different naming systems that might be used.

British family names

Most Christians born in the UK have one or two personal names and then a family name. In Britain and Ireland family names first began to be used after about 1200 when larger numbers of people moved to live in towns. (In villages family names were not really needed, because everyone knew each other). Family names that have their origins in Britain and Ireland have been formed in four different ways. Some family names are based on the first name of an ancestor.
Williamson (son of William)
MacDonald (Mac Donald, son of Donald in Scottish and Irish)
O'Sullivan (descendant of Suileabain in Irish)
Powell (Ap Howell, son of Howell in Welsh)

Some family names are based on appearance or nicknames.
Little
Armstrong

Some family names are based on place names.
Hill
Sunderland

Some family names are based on a person's job
Smith
Baker
Brewer

Caribbean names

Many people whose families come from the Caribbean have family names that come from Britain or Ireland. This is because most Africans who were forced to go the Caribbean as slaves were not allowed to keep their own names. They had to accept names given to them by Europeans. A few people of African-Caribbean origin are now changing their names to African names, to mark their African ancestors.

Jewish names

Jewish names tell us a lot about the movement of Jewish people in Europe and the Middle East.

Most Jewish people living in eastern Europe did not have family names until about 250 years ago. Laws were then passed in Germany, Austria and Russia ordering Jewish people to take family names. This made it easier for governments to collect taxes and make men serve in the army. In Germany, Jewish people were charged money for their new family names. A nice name would cost more than a less attractive name.

Jewish people gor their family names in different ways. Some family names were based on the first name of an ancestor.
Jacobs (from Jacob)
Rosen (from Rosa)

Some family names were based on appearance.
Weiss (white in German)
Gross (big in German)

Some family names were based on place names.
Minsky (from Minsk in Russia)
Berliner (from Berlin in Germany)

Some family names were based on a person's job
Portnoy (from the word for tailor in Russian)
Schneider (from the word for tailor in German and Yiddish)

Jewish people have also changed their names at different times in history. In Russia, Jewish families were forced to hand over their sons to the Russian army. Some young men changed their names to try and avoid serving in the Russian army. For example, in the late 19th century Rabbi Golubchik changed his family name to

Pilavsky to try and avoid serving in the Russian army.

When Jewish people fled as refugees to the UK and USA many of them changed their name. Sometime they translated their family names into the English language. For example' Schneider became Taylor Gutman became Goodman

Sometimes people changed their names to an English name that sounded like their original name. Some newly arrived Jews had their names changed for them by immigration officers who were too lazy to write their names down properly.

Many Jewish people changed their names again when they moved to Israel. Sometimes the new Israeli name was a translation of the old family name

European name	Israeli name
Stein	Even (*meaning stone in Hebrew*)
Goldman	Zahavi (*meaning golden in Hebrew*)

In Israel Jewish people were encouraged to take modern Hebrew names. People who wanted a good career were told that they should change their name.

Ghanaian names

Several different naming systems are used in Ghana. The Ashanti name their children after the day of the week on which the child is born. All the days of the week are named after gods, and have a male and female form.

Day of the Week	Name of God	Male Name	Female Name
Monday/Dwowda	Adwo	Kwadwo	Adua
Tuesday/Benada	Akena	Kobna	Abena
Wednesday/Wududa	Aku	Kwaku	Akua
Thursday/Yaw'da	Ayou	Yau	Yaa
Friday/Fida	Afi	Kofi	Efua
Saturday/Mememda	Amen	Kwame	Ama
Sunday/Kwasida	Assi	Kwasi	Essi

Children are also given additional personal names, one of which is the name of a close relative or family friend. Sometimes the father's name is used as a family name. Women keep their names when they marry.

The Sikh naming system

Most Sikhs have three names: a personal name, a second name and a family surname. For example Sukhvinder Kaur Gill (a woman) Amarjit Singh Gill (a man). But most Sikhs do not use their family surname for religious reasons. Instead all Sikh women use the second name of Kaur (meaning a princess) and all Sikh men use the second name of Singh (meaning a lion). So Sukhvinder Kaur Gill is known as Sukhvinder Kaur and Amarjit Singh Gill is known as Amarjit Singh.

Ethiopian names

Most Ethiopian Christians have three names: a first personal name, followed by a religious name, finally that person's father's first personal name. The religious name is decided by the day that the child is born or baptised. Women usually keep their name when they marry.

Chinese names

Chinese names have three parts: a family name, a middle name and a personal name. The family name is always written first, followed by the middle name and then the personal name.

Family Name	Middle Name	Personal Name
Hoang	Khin	Chan(M)
Ly	Nhi	Mui(F)

Children use the same family name as their father. Women do not change their names on marriage, but are often called their husband's family name when speaking. There about 100 common Chinese family names. The middle name is a second personal name. It may add meaning to the first personal name. The middle name can also be used as a generational name: in some families all brothers, sisters and cousins are given the same middle name. The personal name comes last. Some personal names are specifically male or female, others are not.

In the UK some Chinese people have reversed the order of their names. Chinese people may also have nicknames.

Tamil names

Tamil names are complicated, because Tamils may use two different naming systems.

Two Tamil men's names are
R. Sivanandan
M. V. Vijayapalan

'Sivanandan' and 'Vijayapalan' are the persons' names. They are neither first names nor family names. They would be called Sivanandan or Vijayapalan, and a polite form of address would be Mr Sivanandan and Mr Vijayapalan.

The initials 'R' and 'V' refer to the person's father's name. A few Tamils also have family names, particularly if they have well known and respected ancestors whose name they might wish to remember. Vijayapalan's family name is Malavarayan, and is written down as the first initial.

When a woman marries she will take her husband's name as an initial before her name. Many Tamils also have nicknames or pet names; these are sometimes shortened versions of their name. Vijayapalan and Sivanandan may be called 'Vijay' or 'Siva'.

In both Britain and Sri Lanka some Tamils use the European naming system. School records in the UK are not designed to cope with the Tamil naming system. So some Tamils living in the UK use a first personal name and a family name.

The Spanish naming system

A child will be given a first name, followed by the father's family name and then the mother's family name. Usually only the father's family name will be used when speaking to a person. For example

First name	Father's family name	Mother's family name
Cecilia	Rodriguez	Moreno

She will be known as Cecilia Rodriguez when speaking to her. If Cecilia Rodriguez marries she will carry her father's family name with her and add her husband's father's name in place of her mother's name.

Muslim names

In African Muslim countries a person will have three names. A child will be given three names: a first person name, followed by the father's first name and the grandfather's first name. For example

Amina Fuad Jama (F)
Hassan Abdi Hakim (M)

When a woman gets married she usually keeps her own name. Slightly different naming systems may be used by Iranian, Afghan, Pakistani, Indian and Bangladeshi Muslims.

Activity

UK United?

Time needed: 30 minutes

Each child should choose five gifts they would choose to represent their country to others. The children can draw items, or write them down. Then the lists can be compared, and used to illustrate the multicultural nature of the UK.

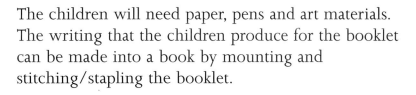

Activity

All about me

The children will need paper, pens and art materials. The writing that the children produce for the booklet can be made into a book by mounting and stitching/stapling the booklet.

In this activity the children are going to produce an autobiographical booklet about themselves. The title of the booklet is All About Me.

The activity should be introduced by the teacher. The children should be given the titles of sections to guide them, but the choice of what goes into the booklet rests with each child. Possible titles for each section might include

- ❧ me ❧ my family ❧ my friends ❧ my house
- ❧ my toys ❧ school ❧ what I do in my spare time
- ❧ what I would like to do in the future

The next six activities examine stereotyping and racism.

Activity

Who influences my ideas?

Time needed: 45 minutes.

This activity aims to help children understand who influences their opinions about controversial issues. The activity can be used after the class has conducted the opinion poll activity on page 120.

Every child should have a large piece of paper and a felt pen.

The teacher should introduce the activity by explaining to the class that we all live in a world where people have many different opinions and ideas. People have different political beliefs and vote for different political parties. People have different ideas about the environment, animal rights, human rights and so on. People have different religious beliefs. People have different ideas about things that go on around them. People have different ideas about who should play for England. The list is endless....

The class is going to consider who influences their ideas. The teacher can take an example to make the activity less abstract. The children should be divided into pairs.

In the middle of the large piece of paper, the children should draw a circle and write me in the middle. Radiating from the middle, the children should write down all the people and things that influence their opinions. The list might include certain friends, parents, television, magazines. Each child should have his or her own 'wheel'.

The class should then come together for a discussion.

Discussion points

❧ Who or what is the most important in influencing your ideas?

❧ Who do you think might influence your ideas about refugees?

Activity

Stereotypes

Time needed: 30 minutes.

The activity aims to show how stereotypes can lead to people developing fixed ideas about groups of people.

The teacher or group leader should write up the following old sayings

"Little girls are made of sugar and spice and all things nice.

Little boys are made of slugs and snails and puppy dogs tails."

As a class, the children should discuss what these rhymes mean. Then the children should be asked if they agree with stereotype that all girls are clean and nice and all boys are dirty and untidy.

The idea of a stereotype can then be explained to the class, using the information provided. Children can be asked if they can think of any other groups that are sometimes stereotyped. This activity can be followed up by reading The Dragon Wore Pink, by Christopher Hope and discussing the story with the class.

Information

Stereotypes and racism

A **stereotype** is a statement about a whole group of people. Ethnic or religious groups can be stereotyped - for example 'all Jews are rich' or 'all Indian people like curry'. A person can be stereotyped because of their sex, for example 'all men are strong'. A person can be stereotyped because of their age too, for example 'all small children are cheeky and dirty'.

Stereotypes are not based on fact and they are often insulting to people. A stereotype can be hurtful because it does not treat a person as an individual. It can also make people believe things about a group that are not true. Stereotypes can also make people frightened of people we do not know. Finally, stereotypes can also lead to people being treated differently because of the group that they belong to.

Treating a person differently because they belong to a certain ethnic group is known as **racism**. Racism can take many forms. Sometimes people can be the victims of violent racist attacks. They can also be treated differently in school and at work.

Sometimes an ethnic group is wrongly blamed for causing a problem. For example refugees are sometimes blamed for causing shortages of housing and jobs. A group or individual person who is blamed for a problem that it did not directly cause is called a **scapegoat**. Ethnic minority groups can be scapegoats. Groups such as refugees can be blamed for causing housing and job shortages.

Dictionary

An **ethnic group** is a group of people who share the same culture and language.

Activity

Inequality

Time needed: 45 minutes.

The activity aims to help children think about individuals or groups of people who are treated unequally. The children will need paper and pens. Recent copies of quality newspapers are needed if working with older children.

The class should be divided into groups of three. In the groups, the children should be asked to write down examples of individuals or groups of people who are treated unequally. The examples can come from school, home, the neighbourhood, nationally or internationally. Newspaper articles can be used to prompt international examples.

The class should then come together. The children's lists can be compared and used as a basis for discussion. Using newspaper, the children can be shown examples of endangered people or refugees being treated unequally.

Discussion point

Do you know of individuals or groups of people treated differently because of their ethnic group?

Activity

Learning from refugee children

The testimonies of Metin, Serpil and Choman and the activity on page 110 can be used in this section as a prompt to examine the way that some refugee chidlren are treated in their new schools.

Activity

Scapegoats

Time needed: 30 minutes.

The activity aims to help children understand scapegoating. The teacher should start by explaining the meaning of the word scapegoat. Then working in groups or as a whole class, the children should be asked if they know of any individuals or groups who are scapegoats in their school or neighbourhood.

The children should be asked the following questions about those who have been made scapegoats.

❥ What were the scapegoats being blamed for?
❥ Was it really their fault?
❥ How do you think it feels to be made into a scapegoat?

Activity

Challenging racism

Time needed: one hour.

The teacher will need to photocopy the following scenario cards. The children should then be divided into groups of three and given one of the scenarios. They should be asked to say what they would do if they were the children in mentioned in the cards.

After the children have read their cards and come to a group decision, the class should come back for a discussion about their decisions.

Scenario cards

Hassan is a classmate of Darren. He is from Somalia. Hassan often gets bullied by a group of boys from another class. One day Hassan hits one of the bullies, but it is Hassan that gets told off and excluded from school. Darren saw the fight and that Hassan did not start it.

What would Hassan do?
What would Darren do?

Jane is in the playground and hears one of her friends telling an Irish joke. Mary is Jane's best friend and she is Irish. Mary hears the joke too.

How would Mary feel?
What would Mary do? What would Jane do?

Alison is walking home from school and hears some children from her class laughing and calling out abuse to a new child in the class. The child is called Sandra and she is a Gypsy from Slovakia. Sandra does not speak much English but she understands that people are making fun of her.

How would Sandra feel?
What would Sandra do?
What would Alison feel?
What would Alison do?

A Somali refugee family have just moved into the flat next door to Alfie, including a boy called Abdi who is the same age as Alfie. Alfie starts to talk to Abdi and learns that Abdi's younger brother was killed in fighting in Somalia. Some other children say that the Somali family have taken a flat that could go to a British family. The other children soon start to bully Abdi when he goes to school.

How would Abdi feel?
What would Abdi do?
How would Alfie feel?
What would Alfie do?

Chapter Seven

Hopes for the Future

Refugees, like any other human beings, have hopes and dreams for the future. They include the ambitions common to all people, but also the hope for peace, the restoration of human rights and the possibility of returning home.

This chapter examines the hopes of individual refugees and through them the solutions to refugee movements, namely ❥ conflict resolution and peace;

❥ the restoration of human rights; and

❥ return or resettlement.

A Bosnian boy returns home from spending three years as a refugee in Scotland HOWARD DAVIES

Activity

Hopes and dreams

The activity aims to get children to examine their own hopes for the future. These can then be compared with the two refugee testimonies in this chapter.

The group will need paper and pens. Everyone will also need copies of the two testimonies.

Children should first work individually. They should spend 20-30 minutes writing about their hopes and ambitions for the future. They should examine areas such as

- my future education
- my career
- hopes for my family
- future relationships and children
- hopes for my country and the world.

After the children have completed their own piece of writing, they should then read the two testimonies in pairs. Each pair should then consider the discussion point.

Discussion point
How did Indira and Lakshmi's hopes for the future differ from yours?

Testimony

Indira's hopes

Indira is a Bosnian Muslim woman. She had a good job in a factory and a small child when she lived in Bosnia. When the war started, her town was overrun with Serbian soldiers. She had to flee. Indira, her husband and child went by bus through Europe and then caught a boat to Sweden. Her second child was born in Sweden and now Indira is hoping to train as a play worker. She does not think she will be able to return to Bosnia to live.

"The world knows we were at war. You have seen only negative pictures of fighting is Bosnia. I don't want you to see me in that way. I would like to relate to others on equal terms. I don't want people to feel sorry for me.

I know it will take time, but one day I hope I can feel welcomed in Sweden. I also hope that all the children in the world will not have the experience of war and nobody should go through the things that we did. I hope that all of us, we should forgive each other. I hope that one day people will understand each other better."

Lakshmi's hopes

Lakshmi is a 12 year old Sri Lankan Tamil girl who left Colombo with her parents and sister when she was seven. She misses her family in Sri Lanka badly.

"I don't know why they have to fight in our country, but I feel sorry for the people in Sri Lanka. Most of all I pray for our family, my Dad's family and my Mum's family.

The difficulty for me is that I don't exactly understand what is going on. Why do they have to fight? It is unfair for the innocent people.

I hope that the fighting stops soon and that everyone can have a normal life and that children in Sri Lanka get the chance to go to school."

Information

Making peace

Refugees need a peace before they are able to think about returning home. In order to make peace in a country that has been at war both politicians and ordinary people have to get together and talk.

Making peace happens at a government level: politicians and other powerful people from opposite sides of the conflict have to get together and solve the problems that have caused the conflict.

Making peace happens between ordinary people: adults and children from opposite sides of the conflict have to get together and solve the local problems that are often part of the conflict.

Making peace does not happen suddenly, you need to carry out several things before you can make peace.

1. Both sides of the conflict have to want to make peace.

2. Both sides of the conflict have to agree to talk to each other.

3. Both sides of the conflict have to agree that the 'other side' are human beings too.

4. Both sides of the conflict have to talk to each other about their needs and problems

5. Both sides of the conflict have to work together to try and find a peaceful solution.

6. Both sides of the conflict may have to give up things, in order to make peace.

7. The peaceful solution has to be supported by as many people as possible.

Peace is needed before refugees can think about returning home.

A peace education project working to bring young Hutu and Tutsi together in Burundi HOWARD DAVIES

Activity

How do we make peace between ourselves?

Time needed: 30 minutes.

The activity is a brainstorming activity which aims to help children understand how they make peace.

The teacher should set the scene. The class should imagine that they are walking home from school with three other friends. One of the friends is very rude about another child's mother. The victim tries to hit the child who has been rude about his mother. What can you do to stop a fight? How should the four friends act to make peace?

As a class, the children should make a list about what they can do to make peace in such a situation and to ensure that everyone continues to be friends.

Activity

Making peace

These two activities aim to show some of the things that children can do to help make peace. For the first activity, you will need to copy the role cards, so that each group of four children has a set of role cards. The children will also need paper and pens.

In the second activity the same role cards will be used. The children are going to make finger or glove puppets and create a puppet show about how children can go about making peace. The class will need material for making puppets, including felt and other cloth, wool, glue, cloth marker pens and so on. The children might also like to make a stage for their puppet show and will need cardboard and paints to do this.

The activity is set in Burundi, a country where there has been major conflict between Tutsi and Hutu people since the 1940s. The conflict erupted into genocide in 1965, 1972, 1988 and 1993 onwards. Tutsi and Hutu people are now being killed every day by political extremists. Over 700,000 people are now refugees and many are displaced in Burundi.

Looking at ways to make peace

The class should be divided into fours. Each group should have a set of role cards. The children should take one of the role cards and read it out to the group. Using the ideas on the role cards as well as their own ideas, the children should use the enclosed worksheet and write down ways that ordinary children can help make peace in Burundi.

continued overleaf

What children can do to make peace

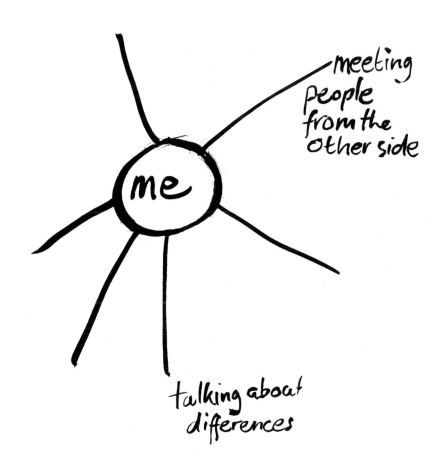

The Puppet Show

The children should work in the same groups. Each group should be given the brief to write a short puppet play to show what the children of the world can do to make peace. The children can take the roles of Justine, Agnes, Christophe and Henri if they wish, or make up their own parts.

Role Cards

Justine lives in a small town in Burundi. She is a Tutsi. Justine is 10 years old. Both her parents are teachers. There are no Hutu families in the street that she lives and very few Hutu children in her school. In the last five years, some of her relatives and friends have taught her to fear Hutu people. One of Justine's aunts was murdered in 1996, by a Hutu neighbour. This made her very frightened.

When Justine was eight years old, she made a new friend at school. Her name was Agnes and she was a Hutu. Agnes persuaded Justine to go along with her to a theatre and music group that meets locally. The theatre group is one place where Hutu and Tutsi children can meet.

At first Justine felt scared to meet Hutu children. But now she is happy to just sit down and talk to them about everyday life. Justine thinks that talking to people about your differences is very important.

Life is not easy at home and school now. At home Justine gets into arguments with her mother about her friendship with Agnes. At school Justine is worried about Agnes. She gets bullied a lot at school. Often Justine tries to stop the bullying.

continued overleaf

Agnes is 10 years old. She is a Hutu. Agnes has four brothers and sisters. She lives in a poor neighbourhood in a small town in Burundi. At her school there are very few Hutu children. Sometimes this is a problem and she gets bullied. But generally she likes school. Agnes wants to be a singer when she is older.

When Agnes was eight years old she made a new friend at school. Her name was Justine and she is a Tutsi. Justine and Agnes now go to the same theatre and music group. The theatre group is one place where Hutu and Tutsi children can meet.

With the help of one of the workers at the theatre group, Agnes has just written a song. The title of the song is 'peace' and it is about a child's hope for peace in Burundi. Agnes is going to perform her song at a concert the group is organising to raise some money to help children living in camps for displaced people in Burundi.

Christophe is 11 years old. Christophe is a Tutsi although, like many families he has some relatives who are Hutu. He has three brothers and sisters. His father works in a shop. The family also own some land outside the town which they use to grow crops.

Christophe likes football and music. He has just joined a theatre and music group. It is one place where Hutu and Tutsi children can meet.

After he joined the theatre and music group he was called a traitor by some of his schools friends because he made friends with Hutu people. He says, "I had no idea that some children had such bad feelings towards others." This has made Christophe more determined and he is thinking of setting up a football team where Hutu and Tutsi children can play together. Together with Henri, he has made a poster about the new football club.

Henri is nine years old. He is a Hutu. Henri lives with his mother and two sisters in a mixed neighbourhood. Henri's father is dead; he was killed by army in 1988. His mother is a dressmaker. Henri attends the same school as Christophe and has friends who are both Hutu and Tutsi. He has just joined a theatre and music group. It is one place where Hutu and Tutsi children can meet.

Henry sometimes sits with his mother and listens to the radio in the evening. He listens to what the politicians say and feels they make things worse. Henry feels that many of them just create hatred between ordinary people. Henri and his mother sometimes argue with their neighbour about the radio programmes.

Henri cannot forget his father's death. He was killed by a Tutsi soldier. Henri has decided that when he is older he wants to study law. He wants to work to protect human rights and stop innocent people being killed.

Tutsi refugees returning to Rwanda

UNHCR

Information

Human rights

Refugees leave their home countries for many different reasons. But all refugees have one thing in common - they have lost their human rights in their home countries. If refugees are to be able to return home, they need to be able to see that their human rights, like to right to safety, are there. But what exactly do we mean by a human right?

A human right is something that all people throughout the world should have. The right to food and clean water are human rights. The right to safety is another human right.

Human rights are based on the idea that all people in the world are equal and deserve fair and equal treatment.

Throughout history many governments and individual people have worked for human rights. After the Second World War, the United Nations was founded. One of its first jobs was to write the Universal Declaration of Human Rights. More recently, the United Nations wrote the 1989 Declaration on the Rights of the Child. This outlines the rights that all children should have in every country that belongs to the United Nations. Of course, many children do not have these rights, but the Charter helps the United Nations and other organisations work for a world where all children do have these rights.

Three generations of a Bosnian refugee family now living in Croatia   UN HCR

Activity

Writing your own human rights charter

Time needed: one hour.

This activity aims to get children thinking about what human rights means in their lives.

The children will need pens and large sheets of paper.

The activity should be introduced by giving an explanation of what is meant by a human right. The information sheet on page 150 can be given to older children to read. The class should then be divided into groups of three. Each small group should then work to produce a ten point charter for children's rights. The children should decided on ten rights that all children in every country should have.

The charters can then be pinned up and compared. They can be used to prompt further discussion.

Discussion point
What rights have young refugees lost?

Activity

Class collage on the 1948 Universal Declaration of Human Rights

The activity aims to familiarise the children with some of the articles of the 1948 Universal Declaration of Human Rights by producing a class collage illustrating the articles.

You will need sugar paper for mounting the paintings. The children will need access to art materials. The articles listed below should be copied and cut up so that every child has one article.

The activity should be introduced to the children, using the information sheet and previous activity if desired. The children are each going to take one of the simplified articles and produce a painting to illustrate the article. The children should also write down the articles on the painting or beside it.

The 1948 Universal Declaration of Human Rights - in simple language

Article 1 All people are born free and equal, and should respect each other.

Article 2 Everyone should have the rights outlined in the Universal Declaration whatever their ethnic group, sex, nationality, religion, political opinion, social group, ability or wealth.

Article 3 Everyone has a right to live in freedom and safety.

Article 4 No-one has a right to make people slaves.

Article 5 No-one should be tortured or punished in a cruel way.

Article 6 The law must treat everyone as people, not objects.

Article 7 Laws must not treat people differently because of their ethnic group, sex, nationality, religion, political opinion, social group, ability or wealth.

Article 8 Everyone has a right to legal help if their rights are ignored.

Article 9 Nobody should be arrested, nor kept in prison or sent away from their country, without a fair reason.

Article 10 Everyone is entitled to a fair and public trial if charged with an offence.

Article 11 If charged with an offence, a person should be considered innocent until it is proved that he or she is guilty.

Article 12 A person has a right to privacy. No-one has a right to say untrue and damaging things about another person.

Article 13 Everyone has a right to travel and live anywhere in their home country. A person also has the right to leave any country, including his or her own, and to return to it.

Article 14 Refugees must be protected in the country to which they have fled.

Article 15 Everyone has a right to a nationality.

Article 16 Every adult person has the right to marry and have children. Men and women have equal rights in marriage, and if they divorce. No-one should be forced to marry against his or her will.

Article 17 Everyone has the right to own property. No-one can take other people's possessions without a fair reason.

Article 18 Everyone has the right to think and believe in what they want, this includes the right to practice a religion.

Article 19 Everyone has the right to express their thoughts, whether by speaking or in writing.

Article 20 Everyone has the right to organise peaceful meetings, and to form groups. But no-one can be forced to join a group.

Article 21 Everyone has the right to take part in the government of his or her country, whether by voting or being an elected member of parliament. Fair elections should be held regularly, and everyone's vote is equal.

Article 22 Everyone has the right to things that meet their basic needs like shelter, health care and enough money on which to live.

Article 23 Everyone has the right to work. Wages should be fair and enable a family to live decently. Men and women should receive the same pay for doing the same work. A person has the right to join a trade union.

Article 24 Everyone has the right to reasonable working hours, rest and paid holidays.

Article 25 Everyone has the right to a decent standard of living. Those who cannot work should receive special help. All children, whether born outside marriage or not, have the same rights.

Article 26. Everyone has the right to education. Primary education should be free and compulsory. A person should be able to continue his or her studies as far as he or she is able. Education should help people live with and respect other people. Parents have the right to choose the kind of education that will be given to their child.

Article 27 Everyone has the right to join in cultural activities, and enjoy the arts. Anything that a person writes or invents should be protected and the person should be able to benefit from its creation.

Article 28 For human rights to be protected there must be order and justice in the world.

Article 29 A person has responsibilities to other people.

Article 30 No government, group or person should ignore the rights set out in the Universal Declaration of Human Rights.

Information

Return or resettlement

Going home

Almost all refugees wish to return home when it is safe. For many refugees this dream will come true. Some refugees go back in small groups, often as just a family. Other refugees return as part of an organised group. The UNHCR is one organisation that helps refugees return home. It gives returning refugees help with transport, packs of material and sometimes money to help in the first months back home. The UNHCR and other organisations may provide seeds and tools so that returning farmers can plant new crops as soon as possible. Returning refugees may also carry home dried food like flour and lentils, to eat while waiting for new crops to grow.

Resettling in another country

Returning home is not possible for some refugees. Wars can go on for many years, and a refugee's home country may not be safe enough. Land mines may prevent refugee farmers returning to their land. Or farms and homes may be occupied by newcomers, preventing refugees from returning. So it is also important to help those refugees who can never return. They will need permanent homes, locally, or in another country. Language teaching and job training may also be provided to help refugees rebuild their lives.

Refugees Who Have Returned		
Group	Dates of Return	Numbers
Mozambicans	1992-1995	1,652,000
Iraqis	1991	1,510,000
Rwandans	1994-	1,300,000
Cambodians	1992-1993	387,000
Bosnians	1996	200,000

This Bosnian man was a refugee for four years. He has just managed to return to his old home and is busy repairing it   HOWARD DAVIES

Farukh Julio's story

Farukh Julio is an 11 year old Mozambican boy. There was fighting in Mozambique from 1964 until 1992. During this time over one million people fled as refugees. The fighting also caused another 4 million Mozambicans to become displaced within their own country.

Farukh Julio was a refugee in Malawi for most of his childhood. Now he has been able to return to his home in Mozambique.

"I was three years old when my family fled into Malawi. My mother has stayed in Malawi, but I came back to Mozambique with my stepfather.

I can still remember the war in Mozambique. I saw someone being killed and I remember that. Sometimes bullets were flying about everywhere. It was the ordinary people that got killed. We were all afraid of being killed at that time. War is very bad.

Since we came back home, we've had many problems because the fields were full of weeds and it was very difficult to clear the land and build new houses. When we went back to the village the old houses were wrecked. We also found some people already living on our farm. So we went to another piece of land - there were no arguments.

We still do not have enough to eat, enough land to farm and enough clothes to wear. Here in school we have no book at all or all the other things that we need for school."

Activity

Going home

Time needed: 45 minutes.

The activity aims to help children think about what refugees may need to be able to return home.

The cards should be copied and cut up. Each group in the class needs a set.

The class should be divided into groups of four. Each group should have a set of cards. The teacher should set the scene: the children should imagine that they are Mozambican refugees who have been living in a refugee camp in Malawi, the neighbouring country. Before thew war in Mozambique, the family owned a small farmers. Now the war has stopped, the refugee family wants to return home.

The children should take it in turns to read the contents of the cards. Then as a group they should decide on the **ten** things that they would most need to be able to return home.

| News from relatives and friends that your home village is now safe. |

| Training for you and your children on how to avoid landmines |

| Some money, about £20 |

| Blankets |

| Five loaves of bread |

| A can for water |

| Plastic sheeting |

| A hoe and other tools to grow crops |

| A clinic in your home village |

| Seeds for planing on your farm |

| A large canvas bag |

| Radio news from the BBC that there is a peace agreement in your home country. |

| Wood, to help you rebuild your house |

| A school in your home village |

| A large sack of flour, cooking oil, dried beans and salt |

| Buses and lorries to take you home |

Information

Landmines

Landmines are small explosives placed in the soil. They are put their during a war. A landmine explodes when a person treads on one. There are over 100 million landmines laid in the soil, mostly in the countries listed here. Every month over 800 people are killed by landmines and many more are injured by them.

Landmines are especially dangerous for children. They are often placed in places where children might play. Landmines also look like interesting toys and often young children pick them up. As children are smaller than adults they are more likely to be killed by a landmine explosion.

Places where landmines are usually laid include

- farmer's fields
- around airports and stations
- at the edges of paths and roads
- in water

When a war finishes, landmines may stop refugees returning to their homes and farms. If there are many landmines in the soil, a farmer will not be able to return to his land and plant crops. So if refugees are going to return, it is important that landmines are removed from farm land.

The Mines Advisory Group is one organisation that takes landmines away, after a war has finished. It also runs classes for children who live in parts of the world where landmines have been laid. The Mines Advisory Group teaches children what landmines look like, and how to avoid treading on them. By doing this, fewer children get killed or injured by landmines.

Countries where most landmines are laid

Afghanistan
Angola
Bosnia
Cambodia
Iraq
Laos
Liberia
Rwanda
Somalia
Sri Lanka
Sudan
Vietnam

A Somali mine clearing team remove land mines   HAMISH WILSON

Activity

Landmines!

Time needed: lesson time and homework time for research.

The activity aims to show children the places that would be out of bounds for them if they lived in a country where landmines were laid. You will need to photocopy the information sheet on landmines.

The activity should be introduced by explaining to children what landmines are and why they may prevent refugees from returning home. The work of Princess Diana could be used to start a discussion. The class will also need to know where landmines are usually laid.

The children are going to plot on a list or draw a map of their journey from school to home and where they go in the evening.

When the children come back to school, the lists and maps can be compared. The teacher or group leader should then highlight the places which would be out of bounds to them if they lived in a country like Bosnia or Somalia, where many landmines are laid.

Chapter Eight

How You Can Help Refugees

This chapter looks at what young people can do to support refugees.

Young refugees, their school friends and families build a shelter in a park to show people the difficulties faced by homeless refugees   KAREN ROBINSON

Activity

If I ruled the world

Time needed: 45 minutes.

This activity aims to get children thinking about what they can do to change things that they consider to be wrong. The activity needs paper and pens.

The class should be divided into groups of three or four. In their groups, the children should imagine that they ruled the world. They should make a list of things that they consider to be wrong or unjust: internationally, nationally and locally in their school or neighbourhood.

When the children have made their lists, they should select one thing on it. Working in the same groups the children should then decide how they would put it right

The class should then come together for a discussion about what the children can actually do to put right what they consider to be wrong.

Activity

Being responsible

Time needed: 45 minutes

In groups or as a whole class the children should think about times during the last year that they have not taken responsibility for doing something, and as a result something bad has happened. It could be something like not stopping a friend being bullied, or letting a little brother or sister get into a dangerous situation.

The children should then read Pastor Martin Niemoller's poem below. Martin Niemoller lived in Germany during the Nazi period. The children should discuss the poem with reference to challenging bullying and racism.

"First they came for the Jews
and I did not speak out
- because I was not a Jew.

Then they came for the communists
and I did not speak out
- because I was not a communist.

Then they came for the trade unionists
and I did not speak out
- because I was not a trade unionist.

Then they came for me
- and there was no-one left
to speak out for me."

Information

How you can help refugees

Refugees depend on your support in many ways. Here are some ideas of things you can do.

Finding out more

Get in touch with refugee organisations to collect more information about refugees.

Inform your friends about refugees by making a school display. You can use the information you have collected from refugee organisations. You might want to show the different aspects of refugees' lives throughout the world in your display. Find out why people become refugees and what help they need in a new country. You could put your display on a noticeboard in the school entrance or in a classroom.

Contact a refugee organisation to invite a refugee speaker to come and talk to your class. You could add what you learn from the speaker to your display.

School assemblies are a good way of informing your friends about refugees. Ask your teacher if you can speak at a school assembly. You might want to write a play for your assembly. Students at the George Mitchell School wrote and performed a short video and drama about refugees called 'Why'. This was later shown to other pupils at their school and to other schools in the area.

You can do many other things to inform your friends and family about refugees. Pupils at Monson Primary School did more than this. They wrote down stories that they knew from home. The stories were collected from the UK, Vietnam, Somalia and Colombia. The children then published their stories in a book called the 'Dooley Alibanger'. A newspaper came to the launch of the story book.

Being responsible for others

Sometimes refugee children are bullied in schools, particularly when they are new. Put yourself

Schools students hand over a petition about refugee children. They have been supported by Griff Rhys-Jones, a comedian   ED CLARK

in their position and think what it would be like to arrive in a new school in anew country. You might want to think about ways that you can stop bullying.

Be a friend to a refugee in your school or neighbourhood. Make sure that refugee children who are new to your school know where to go for lessons and lunch. Your friendship can go a long way in helping a refugee adjust to life in a new country.

Write to an organisation like Oxfam, CAFOD, Christian Aid or Save the Children to find out ways that you can help refugees who are living in the poorer countries of the world.

Join Amnesty International's Junior Urgent Action network to help people who have lost their human rights and may be in great danger.

Fundraising

Organise a fundraising event to collect money for a refugee organisation. You can organise a sponsored walk, football or swimming event to collect money. You will need to plan your fundraising activity and get permission to organise your event. You will also have to design a sponsorship form. A fundraising event can also inform people about the needs of refugees! Norlington School in London raised £220 for refugee organisations by organising a breaktime cake sale and a day when pupils paid a small amount of money not to wear school uniform.

You can collect money for an

organisation that works with refugees in poor countries. You might want to collect money for organisations that work with refugees in the UK.

Write to your local newspaper about your fundraising event. Explain why you are doing this, and what refugees need. You could also contact your local radio station.

Contact an organisation that works with refugees in your town or city. You can find out if they need children's clothes or toys and organise a school collection. Many refugee children arrive a new country with very few belongings. Children at St Mary's School in London collected art materials for refugee children. These were presented to the Refugee Council for use by children at a day centre for refugees.

Remember refugees are ordinary people just like everyone else. It is just that their recent experiences have been difficult and dangerous. They need your support.

Activity

Thinking about what I can do to support refugees

The above information sheet can be used to prompt discussion about a class project to support refugees. The children may want to carry out some of the suggested activities.

Activity

Stopping bullying

Time needed: 45 minutes.

You will need to copy the illustration so that the pairs each have a copy.

The class should be divided up into pairs and given a copy of the illustration. They should be asked what they think is happening in the picture. One child is unhappy and is the target of verbal bullying. The children should put themselves in the position of the bystander and then be asked what they would do to stop the bullying.

Activity

Writing a guide
to my school for a new pupil

Time needed: at least two hours and homework time.

The children will need paper and felt pens.

The activity can be introduced by asking the children to think back to their first day at school and what it felt like. They children can be asked if they had any particular difficulties, such as not knowing where things are located.

The children should be told that they are going to make a guide for pupils who are new to the school. The guide might include

- a map of the neighbourhood
- a plan of the school
- a timetable for the school day
- what you will need to bring with you to school
- information about homework and uniform
- and any other points the children would like to include.

The guide can be made in the form of a stapled booklet. A few schools have actually printed guides written by pupils and given them to new children. The activity can be followed up by considering what a pupil who is new to the UK might need to know that is different to a child who has already been living in the country. The class could also look at ways of presenting information to children who do not speak much English.

Activity

Making a welcome poster for my school

Time needed: one hour.

The children will need sugar paper, cartridge paper, felt pens and paints. You will also need to photocopy the information below which lists 'welcome' in different languages.

Many schools display welcome posters in different languages. Children can make their own welcome posters. The enclosed information can be used to help the children

Information

Welcome in different languages

Welcome

English

Croeso

Welsh

Failte

Irish

Bienvenus

French

Bem-Vindos

Portuguese

Bienvenidos

Spanish

Mirë seerdhët

Albanian

Jame zamangas tumen ilestyr

Romany

Dobro došli

Serbo-Croat (Bosnian)

Hoş Geldiniz

Turkish

Xêr hatin

Kurdish (Kurmanji)

به خێر بێن

Kurdish (Sorani)

مرحبا بكم

Arabic

Soo dhawow

Somali

እንቋዕ፡ ደሓን፡መጻእኩም።

Tigrinya

Karibu

Swahili

Ilǒ lá

Ibo

E kuabo

Yoruba

እንኳን ደህና መጣች

Amharic

வணக்கம்

Tamil

Hoan Nghênh

Vietnamese

Information

The Amnesty Junior Urgent Action Network

Amnesty International runs the Junior Urgent Action Network for young people aged 8-12 who are interested in helping people in dangerous situations throughout the world.

About Amnesty International

Amnesty International campaigns for human rights in every country of the world. It believes that people detained for their political or religious beliefs should be released and that all prisoners should have fair trials. Amnesty International also works to end the death penalty, torture and other cruel treatment of prisoners. The disappearance and murder of people by soldiers is another thing that Amnesty International campaigns against.

Amnesty International's headquarters are in London and it now has over one million members in 150 different countries. Members write letters to governments and other groups that do not respect people's human rights. Members also try and inform other people about human rights and raise funds to help Amnesty International carry on its work.

The Amnesty International Junior Urgent Action Network sends out monthly appeals to young people aged 8-12 years. With the help of an adult (usually a teacher, parent or friend) the Junior Member writes letters to help people whose lives are in danger because their human rights are not respected. Junior members receive information about the person and their home country.

Young people write letters to help people in many different countries. Recently, Junior Members have written letters to help a nine year old boy beaten by the police in China and a 14 year old boy who was badly treated by the police in the Federal Republic of Yugoslavia.

You can get information about the Amnesty International Junior Urgent Action Network by writing to

Junior Urgent Action Coordinator

Amnesty International (UK)
99-119 Roseberry Avenue
London EC1R 4RE.

Activity

The water activity for fundraising

The activity aims to help children develop their organisational and communication skills.

The children will need paper to design sponsorship forms, and some buckets for the activity. Prior to carrying out the activity, the teacher should have contacted an organisation that works with refugees in poor countries. It might provide a speaker or promotional literature on its work.

The activity should be introduced by explaining that girls and women living in the refugee camps in Sudan, Somalia and Kenya walk an average of 4.5 kilometres every day to collect water for their families. The group is going to walk 4.5 kilometres carrying a bucket of water, to raise money for work with refugees in poor countries.

The children will need set a day for the walk and to plan the route that participants will take. They could walk around a football pitch or the playground, for example. The route must be safe, and away from roads. The children may have to get permission for the walk if they are going to use a football pitch.

The children will need to meet to design sponsorship forms. They must have a contact name and address on them, and give a brief explanation of the uses of the money.

The children may like to publicise their fundraising activity in the local paper or on local radio. They can draw attention to the problems faced by many refugees in poor countries, and also the way that organisations are working to support them.

Children should collect sponsorship from family and friends. On the day of the walk they will need buckets and access to a tap.

Someone should be appointed to be responsible for collecting in the money.

After the walk the children can discuss how they felt, and what they learned from the activity.

Further Resources

General Issues / Human Rights

Amnesty International Report 1997
For teachers. This is an annual report which gives summaries of human rights conditions in all parts of the world.

Amnesty International (UK) (1997)
Our World, Our Rights
A teacher's resource introducing human rights to primary aged children.

Hewitt, Maggie and Harris, Annie (1998)
Talking Time: using real people's life histories
An oral history resource, published by Learning by Design

Highfield Junior School/Gulbenkian Foundation (1996)
Changing our School: promoting positive behaviour
A book of one school's activities and experiences that they used to challenge bullying.

Jewish Council for Race Equality (1998)
Jewish Perspectives on Racism: a primary school resource

Minority Rights Group (1998)
Forging New Identities: young refugee and migrant students tell their stories

Oxfam (1997)
Making Peace
A teaching resource about conflict and reconciliation.

Refugee Council (1998)
Why Do They Have to Fight: refugee children's stories from Bosnia, Kurdistan, Somalia and Sri Lanka.

Rutter, Jill (1994)
Refugee Children in the Classroom
Trentham Books
A background book for teachers and others who are working with refugee students.

Save the Children Fund (1993)
Children: a right to refuge
A free leaflet about refugee children.

Save the Children (1995)
Children at War
SCF, London
A free leaflet giving useful background information.

UNHCR (1994)
Refugee Children
UNHCR, London.
A free leaflet for students.

Refugees in History
Cohn, Frederick (1990)
Signals: A Young Refugee's Flight from Germany in 1930s
United Writers Publications
An exploration of the feelings of two young refugees as they travel to Britain

Ethnic Communities Oral History Project
Passport to Exile: the Polish Way to London
Polish people tell their experiences; suitable for students. Available from the Ethnic Communities Oral History Project.

Ethnic Communities Oral History Project
Ship of Hope

The story of 4,000 Basque children evacuated to London in 1936.

Geras, Adele (1989)
Voyage
Hamish Hamilton
The story of refugees fleeing Eastern Europe at the beginning of the 20th century.

Gwynne, Robin (1985)
Huguenot Heritage
Routledge and Kegan Paul
A background book for teachers.

Kent Arts and Libraries
Anne Frank in the World
Teacher's Pack. Available from the Anne Frank Educational Trust

Kerr, Judith (1971)
When Hitler Stole Pink Rabbit
A novel about escaping Nazi Germany, written by a refugee who came as a child.

Kerr, Judith (1973)
The Other Way Around
What happened after Anna arrived in the UK.

Landau, Ronnie (1992)
The Jewish Holocaust: A Universal Experience
IB Tauris, London
A book of background information, of great use to teachers.

Levy, Herbert
Voices from the Past
A Testimony of a child who came on the Kindertransporte. Available from the Anne Frank Educational Trust

Rutter, Jill (1994)
Jewish Migrations
Wayland
A book for students aged 11-15

Serraillier, Ian (1956)
The Silver Sword
Puffin
A story of four refugee children, suitable for 11-15 year olds.

Supple, Carrie (1993)
From Prejudice to Genocide: Learning about the Holocaust
Trentham Books
A background book for teachers

White, Irene
I Came As A Stranger
The story of a young refugee who fled to escape Nazi persecution
Available from the Anne Frank Educational Trust

White, Irene
And So We Shall Gather
Further memoirs of a young refugee.
Available from the Anne Frank Educational Trust.

Angola

Christian Aid (1995)
Angola: Highlight Sheet
A useful factsheet for teachers.

Ed Warner, Rachel (1995)
Voices from Angola
Minority Rights Group
A collection of testimonies of refugee children.

Bosnia

Filipovic, Zlata (1994)
Zlata's Diary
Methuen.

The diary of a girl growing up in Sarajevo.

Rady, Martyn (1994)
The Break Up of Yugoslavia
Wayland
A book for students aged 12-16
Refugee Council (1998)
The Boy with the Empty Pot
A folk story in Bosnian and English for infant schools.

Silver, N (1995)
The Death of Yugoslavia
BBC Books
An excellent background book for teachers

Silverman, R. (1997)
A Bosnian Family.
Lerner Publications, Minneapolis
A reader for 9-11 year olds

Burundi and Rwanda
Oxfam (1994)
Rwanda: Caught in Conflict
Leaflets for students and teachers.

Congo (Zaire)

Refugee Council (1998)
The Leopardess and Her Cubs
A folk story in English and French

Ed Warner, Rachel (1995)
Voices from Zaire
Minority Rights Group
A collection of testimonies of refugee children

Eritrea

Christian Aid (1994)
Eritrea: Africa's Newest Country
A primary school pack.

Ed Warner (1991)
Voices from Eritrea
Minority Rights Group
A collection of testimonies of
refugee children.

Guatemala

Burr, Margaret (1992)
**We Have Always Lived Here: the
Maya of Guatemala**
A teaching resource.

Kosova

Refugee Council (1998)
The Man Who Understood Animals
A bilingual folk story in English
and Albanian

The Kurds

King, John (1992)
The Kurds
Wayland Publishers
A reading book for 11-16 year
olds.

Laird, Elizabeth (1991)
Kiss the Dust
Heinemann.
A story about an Iraqi Kurdish
girl forced to flee from her
home to London.

Refugee Council (1998)
Sengilo, Mengilo
A folk story in English, Kudish
(Kurmanji) and Turkish.

Ed Warner, Rachel, (1991)
Voices from Kurdistan
Minority Rights Group
A collection of testimonies of
refugee children.

The Palestinians

McDowall, David (1995)
The Palestinians
Minority Rights Group
Excellent background
information for teachers.

Somalia

Buxton, C. and Abdi, S (1997)
A Journey Through Somalia
A book about Somali culture,
written for primary school
children. Published by Learning
by Design.

Lewis, I.M. (1993)
Understanding Somalia
HAAN Associates
An invaluable teacher
background to Somalia.

Refugee Council (1998)
The Deceiver.
A Somali folk story illustrated
by Abdulkadir Muhamed Jama.

Sulieman, Anita (1991)
**Somali Studies: Land of the People,
Early History, Stories from the Land
of Punt, Somali Nomads, Food and
Somali People of the Horn of Africa**
HAAN Associates.
Six booklets plus teaching
notes.

Ed Warner, Rachel (1991)
Voices from Somalia
Minority Rights Group
A collection of testimonies of
refugee children.

Wilkes, Sybella (1994)
One Day We Had to Run
Evans Brothers
A book for children aged 9-15,
with the stories of refugee

children from Somalia, Sudan
and Ethiopia. Highly
recommended.

Sri Lanka

Refugee Council
The Woodcutter
A folk story in English and
Tamil.

Sudan

Oxfam (1995)
Sudan: An Oxfam Country Profile
A background for teachers,
available from Oxfam.

Ed Warner, Rachel (1995)
Voices from Sudan
Minority Rights Group
A collection of testimonies of
refugee children.

Wilkes, Sybella (1994)
One Day We Had to Run
See Somalia.

Uganda

Ed Warner, Rachel (1995)
Voices from Uganda
Minority Rights Group
A collection of testimonies of
refugee children

Viet Nam

Strachan, Ian (1980)
Journey of a Thousand Miles
Methuen
A novel about the journey of a
Vietnamese refugee

Organisations

P = organisations which provide publications on refugees and related issues.
E = organisations which have educational programmes working with young people.

Action Aid Collaborative
Learning Project
Hamlyn House
London N19 5PG
0171-281-4101
E

Amnesty International - UK
99-119 Rosebery Avenue
London EC1R 4RE
0171-814-6200
P E A worldwide human rights organisation. Amnesty Interantional produces a wide range of published material and is engaged in human rights education.

Anne Frank Educational Trust
PO Box 432
Bushey
Herts WD2 1QU
P E

Catholic Fund for Overseas Development
2 Romero Close
Stockwell Road
London SW9 9TY
0171-739-7900
P E

Christian Aid
PO Box 100
London SE1 7RT
0171-620-4444
P E

Commission for Racial Equality
Elliot House 10 Allington Street
London SW1 5EH
0171-828-7022

Development Education Association
3rd Floor
29-31 Cowper Street
London EC1R 4AP
0171-490-8108
The DEA is the umbrella group of British development education centres. It will give you the address of your nearest development education centre if needed.

Development education centres They are usually a good source of educaitonal material about refugees and related issues. Many development education centres have libraries and will lend teachers educational materials. The Development Education Association (0171-490-8108) will put you in touch with your local development education centre.

At present development education centres operate in Ambleside, Ashburton/Devon, Aylesbury, Birmingham, Bournemouth, Bristol, Cambridge, Chelmsford, Cheltenham, Chesterfield, Colchester, Derby, Dudley, Hull, Lancaster, Leamington Spa, Leeds, Leicester, London, Malvern, Manchester, Marlborough, Middlesborough, Milton Keynes, Newton Abbot, Northwich, Norwich, Nottingham, Oxford, Preston, Reading, Settle, Sheffield, Winchester, Yeovil, York, Bangor, Llandidloes, Aberdeen, Dingwall, Dundee, Edinburgh, Falkirk, Belfast and Derry.

The Equality Learning Centre
LVSC
356 Holloway Road
London N7
0171-700-0100
Ethnic Communites Oral

History Project
The Lilla Huset
191 Talgarth Road
London W6 8BJ
0181-741-4076

Haan Books
PO Box 607
London SW16 1EB

Irish Refugee Council
Arran House
35 Arran Quay
Dublin 7
P E

Jewish Council for Race Equality
33 Seymour Place
London W1N 6AT
0181-455-0896
P E

Learning by Design
Tower Hamlets Professional Development Centre
English Street
London E3 4TA
0181-983-1944

Midlands Refugee Council
5th Floor, Smithfield House
Digbeth
Birmingham B5 6BS
0121-242-2200

Minority Rights Group
379 Brixton Road
London SW9 7DE
0171-978-9498

National Committee for Development Education
16-20 South Cumberland Street
Dublin 2
Tel: 01-662-0866
Coordinates development education work in Ireland
North East Refugee Service
19 Bigg Market
Newcastle upon Tyne NE1 1UN
Tel: 0191-222-0406

Northern Refugee Centre
Jew Lane
off Fitzalan Square
Sheffield S1 2BE
Tel: 01742-701429
This organisation has a resource centre

Oxfam
274 Banbury Road
Oxford OX2 7DZ
Tel: 01865-311311
P E

Oxfam has a youth and education department and also regional offices carrying out educational work in Cardiff, Glasgow and London.

The Save the Children Fund
Mary Datchelor House
17 Grove Lane
London SE5 8RD
P E

The Save the Children Fund has an education department and regional offices.

Scottish Refugee Council
2nd Floor, 73 Robertson Street
Glasgow G2 8QD
Tel: 0141-221-8793

and 43 Broughton Street
Edinburgh EH1 3JU
Tel: 0131-557-8083

UNICEF UK
55 Lincon's Inn Fields
London WC2A 3NB
Tel: 0171-405-5592
P E

UNHCR, UK Branch Office
21st Floor, Millbank Tower
21-24 Millbank
London SW1P 4QP
Tel: 0171-828-9191
P

Welsh Refugee Council
Unit 8, Williams Court
Trade Street
Cardiff CF1 5DQ
Tel: 01222-666250

Refugee Council
3 Bondway
London SW8 1SJ
Tel: 0171-582-6922
P E

The Refugee Council supports asylum-seekers and refugees in Britain and campaigns on refugee issues throughout the world. It publishes a wide range of information and there is a specialist service for schools, including

✦ answering individual requests for information from students and teachers
✦ producing publications for use in the classroom, by youth groups and for teachers
✦ providing in-service training about refugees and educational provision for refugee students
✦ giving advice and curriculum support to teachers.

Refugee Community Organisations

There are over 250 active refugee organisations in Britain. They are self help groups working with refugees from many different regions and countries, including

Afghanistan
Algeria
Angola
Bosnia
Chile
China
Colombia
Czechoslovakia
Eritrea
Ethiopia
Ethiopia (Tigrayans and Oromo)
Ghana
Iran
Iran (Armenians)
Iraq
Iraq (Assyrians)
Iraq (Kurds)
Ivory Coast
Nigeria
Poland
Rwanda
Sierra Leone
Somalia
Somalia (Bravanese)
Sri Lanka
Sudan
Turkey
Turkey (Kurds)
Uganda
Togo
Viet Nam
Zaire

The Refugee Council will provide addresses of these organisations and can put teachers in contact with refugee speakers.